SENTAURA RISING

RETURN OF THE ANCIENT CREATOR FREQUENCY

UNLOCKING YOUR UNIQUE CREATOR CODES
AND RISING AS A SOVEREIGN BEING

NATALI BROWN
GEORGINA CURNOW
SHARLENE ELLIS
KIMBERLEY JADE PIPE

SENTAURA PUBLISHING

Copyright © 2022 Natali Brown and Sentaura Publishing

All rights reserved. Apart from any fair dealing for the purposes of brief quotations in articles or speeches, research, private study, or review as permitted by the most recent Copyright Law, no part of this book may be reproduced in any form, mechanical, photographic or electronic without prior written permission from the publisher.

The information given in this book should not be treated as a substitute for professional medical advice. Always consult a medical practitioner. Any use of information in this book is at the reader's discretion and own risk. Neither the authors nor the publisher or any parties associated with the publishing of this book can be held responsible for any loss, claim or damage arising out of the use, or misuse, of the suggestions made, the failure to seek medical advice or for any material produced or mentioned on third party websites and other publications.

Both UK and US grammar and spelling have been used to format this book.

Image and Cover Design by Natali Brown

Interior Design, Editing and Formatting by Natali Brown

SENTAURA® is a registered trademark

ISBN : 978-0-646-73222-0

BOOK 1

For all the brave humans

who are shining their light

for love and truth

We see you

We love you

You are here on this Earth for a reason

Stay true to the soft whispers from your Soul

CONTENTS

CONTENTS v
PREFACE i
   Leiliyah Nevayah i
   How to use this book ix
INTRODUCTION xi
   Return Of the Ancient Creator Frequency xi
   Origins of Sentaura xiv
A SOUL CALLING FROM THE DIVINE 1
   The Birthing of a Name 1
   How to Unlock the Potential of Your Soul 4
   Returning To the Light of Source 12
   The Return of The Seraphim Creation Angels 16
   Connecting With Our Soul Family and Monadic Wisdom 25
   Creating Golden Codes of Light 27
   The Soul Seed Tree of Creation 31
   Meeting The Woman with Pure White Hair 34
   Love and Reflection Practice 40
   Quantum Rings of Velocity 42
   Why 'Merging' with the Higher Self is Key to Our Evolution 49

    Goodbye Illusions and Hello New Me 53

    Coming Back to the "TRUE YOU" 60

    Acknowledge When Your Soul Gifts Come 'Online' 64

    Flowing With Life, Not Against It 66

    True Joy Comes from Loving Yourself Fiercely 68

    New Beginnings Are Afoot! 71

NATALI BROWN 2

A GLIMPSE INTO MY WONDERFUL COSMIC WORLD
THAT IS SENTAURA 76

    Embodying My Divine Sovereignty 85

    Out Of This World Initiation Experiences.......................... 89

    Organic Multi-faceted Event 94

    Healing our Blessed Mother Earth 100

    Divine Gifts Received with a Gracious Heart 104

    My First Time Hands-On Sentaura Healing 108

    How Has Sentaura Influenced My Life and BEing? 111

    And Now to Close This Magical Portal 116

GEORGINA CURNOW 118

FINDING MY VOICE AND MY TRUTH.............................. 120

    Listening To the Guidance from My Soul 124

    How Sentaura Changed My Life for Good 126

    Healing My Ancestral Line...129

IGNITE YOUR FIRE - A Ceremony to Bring in The New 132

The Emotional Pain Body and Sentaura Royal Creator Key Code of Joy™ 134

Healing In the Moment 137

Healing My Heart 138

Delving into the Akashic Records 141

Healing The Land with Sentaura 143

The Orion Initiation 147

Unicorns and Angels 152

My Experience with Sentaura Distance Healing 154

How I Work with Sentaura Now 158

SHARLENE ELLIS 160

SENTAURA CALLED ME FROM THE DEPTHS OF MY STRUGGLE 162

Being an Empath 167

Following The Call of My Heart 169

Rising Into the Light, a Deep Process 170

Awakening The Goddess Within 173

My Star Mother and Soul Family 174

The Wild Woman 176

The Abundance Code 177

The Fairies 178

Rays of Light 181

Our Special Healing Place 182

New Guides 186

Happy and Free 188

I Will Forever Be Grateful for This Woman 190

How I combine Kinesiology with Sentaura Healing 192

Earth Healing 194

The Alchemic Dance Floor 196

Sentaura Changed my Life 197

Mould Client 200

Sexual Trauma Client 202

The Poisoned Dog 204

Working with Sentaura is Truly Fulfilling 205

KIMBERLEY JADE PIPE 206

Dedicated To 208

Write A Review 208

PREFACE

Leiliyah Nevayah

I was born on the conscious day of universal love, at the end of the zodiac month of Pisces, and at the beginning of Aries.

For as long as I can remember I've felt the unencumbered pulse of love move through me. Little did I know that this burning passionate spark of love and devotion would be what ignited my highest soul mission and purpose in my forties. It would be the driving force behind my work to help humanity access our capacity to trust in the authority of our hearts and return to love.

I always felt different and would see the world around me in a different way.

As a child I would see the beauty in human beings, I could tap into their true essence and amplify that light within them. The light within me would be reflected within them and it would be as if their troubles and shadows would simply dissolve. It stayed with me throughout my life and would sometimes feel as if every ounce of my expression was an outpouring of love.

At times waves of this energy raged through my body as I matured, and I wasn't always sure what to do with it.

As I began to embody the creator frequency of Sentaura in 2018 I could feel my energy 'power up' a thousandfold and my body go extremely hot each time this pure stream of divine and unconditional love of God's Creator energy flowed through me.

Spirit gave me my spirit name, Leiliyah Nevayah, and told me that the time would come for me to share it with the world as it carries a vibration of ancient remembrance for those who hear it.

I began to tap into higher streams of Christ consciousness, was seeing many variations of sacred geometry light codes and sometimes I felt as if I 'swallowed' a scientific journal. I would channel things I had never heard of before—I could feel the pulse of various vibrations, began to channel different frequencies, and see and discern equations, formulae and universal concepts.

I could see micro-particles in the body, performed 'psychic surgery', learnt about organic technologies and energetic connections beyond the body. I worked with the vibration of colour from early on in my life and this became more amplified. I would remove entities and denser energies in an instant.

I was shown how to work with a technology which I called Crystal Light Body Technology™ to attune or 'switch on' or 'switch off' crystals in our light bodies and how to use this technology in co-creation with the frequency of Sentaura. Crystals are record keepers or "wisdom keepers" as Spirit calls them and they each have a very specific function to calibrate and upgrade our light body system.

I explored working with the healing frequencies of sound and would spend hours toning and singing light language whilst playing my crystal bowls or drum and could feel the interplay of different sounds. I could see timelines as golden threads and was able to merge and shift them.

I was shown how to work with solar energy from our sun to rejuvenate my body and would teach this to clients and students. Light language or Soul Speak as I call it flowed from me in waves of love. Ancestors would speak through me and let themselves be heard.

I would visit different realms during meditation journeys and meet with the beings there whilst listening to them share their wisdom. I established a deep connection with Mother Gaia, the elements, elementals and dragons—they became my friends and protectors and shared their codes with me.

I was taught by the universal beings of love and guardians of divine wisdom—Jesus, Ascended Masters, The Seraphim Creation Angels, Angelic Realms and Cosmic Beings of Light were all contributing to and supporting my schooling. Each time my cosmic teachers would share something with me they would ask me to do my own research, practice and see results for myself, and so I got to trust my own multi-dimensional channelling abilities.

There was a lot of what I experienced that I could not share with my husband, my children, or my friends. To me, it made perfect sense but I found it difficult to eloquently explain all that I was experiencing.

My body went through different stages of change and I found that I no longer ate or craved certain food. I would lose weight and during energetic upgrades, I would gain weight. After Sentaura initiations I would feel so hungry due to the amount of energy channelled. I could not stomach coffee any longer and was guided to drink water with a high PH balance and consumed a lot of fruit and vegetables. I spent a lot of time in nature, walking on the beach, connecting with my Spirit Guides and the elements of nature, and grounding my energy. All I could do was be present during this change and accepted each stage of what I was going through.

Only later in life, would I find out that my *Gene Key is 25 and that my biggest gift in this life is acceptance of all that I am. According to this Gene Key, my biggest shadow is transmuting my own pain and transcending the suffering of all humanity. It's interesting that most of my work in my thirties and forties related to this.

Indeed, I've been on a profound healing journey. I had to find my true self and accept my soul mission and that came with its own challenges. At times of my own healing, deeply sitting in my own shadows, it felt like an enormous undertaking and I wasn't sure how I was going to share what I knew with humanity. All I knew was that it was important and that I had to get this work out to the world.

My Spirit Guides kept encouraging me and assisting me through each step of my healing journey. I began to trust instead of questioning my own abilities and that's when I had breakthrough after breakthrough which led to where I am today teaching Sentaura students all over the world.

Even though I teach healing arts and spiritual sciences I am also always a student in this Earth School. I would not be able to do the work with Sentaura unless I did the deep work to face my fear and transmute my own shadows. There is no leader who can say they have never walked through their shadows to find their light.

I shared Sentaura with a select group of people at first. I could feel the sacredness of this work and treated the alchemical workings of this frequency with the utmost respect. I would start with one-on-one healing for closest friends and family and then move on to workshops, sacred healing gatherings, online events, courses, retreats and festivals. The results were incredible.

When people ask me about Sentaura, I would say: "Would you like to experience it?" Without receiving the loving and healing frequency of Sentaura you would not know how it can help you.

During gatherings, I would invite people to surrender to the love and freedom of the Sentaura frequency. It was as if this invitation gave people permission to let go of all that they were not.

These gatherings were euphoric, the feeling of unconditional love and the potency of The Seraphim Creation Angels was like a beautiful blanket wrapped around us.

Waves of light would roll over and through people and there were times I felt as if I wanted to explode with the immense power of love that was radiating from my heart. People would naturally begin to move with the energy flowing through them as they danced and you could see the bliss and joy on their faces.

In this state of bliss, our masculine, too structured way of being would take a back seat as Sentaura amplified the profound power of the feminine and moved it through us like liquid gold. I was in awe of the human vessel and the vessel of life itself where we got to grow, flow, create, transform, generate, inspire and birth ourselves into being.

During one full moon gathering, Spirit showed me how we could breathe light into the body to upgrade our bodies and activate our Gold Light Body and so the Sentaura Breath of Light Practice™ was born.

I would receive new information in the form of visions, and telepathic downloads. I felt a deep remembrance as I would hear, see, sense and experience these messages and energies in my whole being.

I was co-creating with the Divine and it was beautiful.

Working with my divine guides The Seraphim Creation Angels, I experienced an equal measure of bliss, transmutation, and profound transformation and my Guides alluded to the fact that the work with Sentaura would take commitment beyond human comprehension.

Those who enrolled for my Sentaura Healing Practitioners training listened to their deep soul calling and jumped into this work with an open heart not truly knowing what to expect but they trusted me.

I am so grateful to these women for believing in me. Spirit said: "Your first group of Sentaura Healing Practitioners will be healing anchors of light and all who follow in their footsteps will strengthen this light and build upon this solid foundation anchoring their own light".

The Divine Feminine would lead and the Divine Masculine will rise to meet Her.

I began to initiate and guide a community of powerful healers and visionaries all over the world—sovereign heart leaders of the New Earth who were here to pave the way for humanity, sharing their own unique soul gifts in a way only they can.

They are the way showers of our time during the Golden Age of Gaia. They unlocked within them the wisdom of Creation, the wisdom and love of God, our Creator. They will go on to ignite the sovereign hearts of humanity so it can ripple to future generations.

They are the women in this book and transcribed in the pages are their personal accounts of their phenomenal journey with Sentaura.

I have such a deep love for these beautiful souls. They are my Soul Sisters. There were many initiations where my tears flowed freely in gratitude for these sacred hearts and powerful healers, goddesses, and warriors of light.

They are emissaries of the light, keepers of the Earth and so are all the Sentaura Healers who will follow in their footsteps.

This book is a gateway to accessing your most beautiful self and your unique abilities. I share with you snippets of my own story so you may begin to see the magnificence of your soul integrated into your human existence.

Being sovereign is claiming back your divine connection to all that is. It's remembering how interconnected you are as you weave and play and create during your Earth experience.

Life doesn't happen to you, it happens because of you.

It is truly a wonderful time to be alive and my hope is that you will follow your free-spirited human nature and the truth of your heart as I share with you pieces of the puzzle as a living temple for light and love.

How to use this book

Create a sacred space and carve out time for you to read.

Light a candle and surround yourself with your favourite crystals.

Take a deep breath in and set the intention to be open to receive soul activations, messages and healing that is for your highest good and the highest greatest good of all.

Grab your journal to answer the prompts which will help you navigate the musings of your mind.

If you do, this book will bring you valuable insights.

You may even discover more about your own gifts and find your soul wisdom being activated.

If you're brave enough to open your heart and look within, much will be revealed and transformed as you journey through the stories in this book.

Do not be afraid to face your shadows. Do not be afraid that you will lose your power or be afraid of the magnificence of your own power. For you will in fact ignite your fire and gain the greatest power of all—love born through vulnerability and humility.

The most extraordinary warriors and leaders possess these qualities.

Beloved, within the fires of love, you will once again regain the greatest softness, your innate spiritual power, the divine alchemy of God, and your purest and brightest light.

*Gene Key 25 is encapsulated within the Codon Ring of Humanity according to Founder of Gene Keys Richard Rudd. The Sacred wound at the heart of humanity and the reason for all of our suffering can be unlocked by the Gene Keys that make up this Codon Ring.

As one of the most complex codon groups, each of the six Gene Keys in this group represents an archetypal aspect of the human story, together encapsulating all the mythic elements of what it means to be a human being.

Wounded from the outset (25), you must do battle with your shadows (38), overcome the limitations of your mind (17), surrender your need to control life (21) and find your true self (10) before you can awaken (51). You can see from this very profound grouping how deeply bonded we humans are by the same basic dramas. Many of the Gene Keys in this codon group concern love and the human capacity to trust in the authority of the heart. The very blueprints of our human destiny and the future evolution of humankind lie coiled within this ring, along with the six essential human attributes truly natural and inherent to our species.

https://genekeys.com/gene-key-25/

INTRODUCTION

Return Of the Ancient Creator Frequency

During a channelled session in 2018 Spirit told Natali Brown (Leiliyah Nevayah) that she would activate within her an Ancient Creator Frequency. They shared that her unique energetic make-up, soul codes and *Gold Print would pave the way for her to channel and transmit the intelligence of the ancient creator and healing Source frequency of Sentaura.

With the guidance of her Spirit team, she created a multi-dimensional energy healing system merging frequency work, light language, sound, and sacred geometry light codes, all designed to heal, activate, upgrade and recalibrate our human body's DNA Genetic Code and Crystalline Gold Light Body (also known as the Christic Body).

Over the next two years, she went through a profound initiation process with The Seraphim Creation Angels, Ascended Masters, Guardians, Councils of Light and Archangels until they told her in early 2020 that the teachings of Sentaura were ready to be introduced to humanity.

She was running a healing and spiritual coaching and mentoring practice at the time, teaching Reiki and doing healing sessions and readings as a multi-dimensional channel for Source bringing through teachings and wisdom from the Divine.

Natali received the divine directive from Source to initiate those who are ready to hear the call from Sentaura for our own personal evolution, the evolution of our planet and humanity's highest soul ascension, equally serving the greater good and the multiverse through our expansion.

In January 2020 Natali was sitting at her kitchen table working on the details of her first Healing Practitioner Program for Sentaura when she saw what she now knows were pieces of her life puzzle, flashes of important moments in her life being shown to her in a vision—people, experiences, situations which all led her to this exact moment.

After the vision, she began to more deeply embody the work she was here to do with the Divine. She received many downloads from The Seraphim Creation Angels and various other Beings of Light in the form of sacred geometry code, light language, sound alchemy and channelled Source wisdom. She would spend hours writing and drawing all that was shared with her.

She was told that she is a wisdom keeper and teacher of LOVE and that her work with Sentaura would be her life's work and highest mission and purpose. They disclosed that many Beings of Light had been working behind the scenes over many lifetimes, including her Higher Self, to bring the wisdom of Source and its purity back to humanity at this exact time of human consciousness.

Over the years she worked in co-creation with the Seraphim Creation Angels, Jesus, Archangel Metatron, Saint Germain, Guardians and various other cosmic beings and Mother Gaia.

She would see flashes of the most beautiful sacred geometry codes in her mind and could feel the pure frequency of these codes vibrating in her cells. These codes would function as keys to unlock specific soul aspects and upgrade the human DNA genetic profile.

She drew the first of a series of twenty-four Sentaura Royal Diamond Creator Key Codes™ and on 2 July 2021 Natali began a seven-month journey initiating her first students as Sentaura Healing Practitioners and Cosmic Alchemists of Light™.

In her Mystery School, The Divine Light Academy of Ascension Natali initiates her students, so they uncover and unlock their own unique abilities and soul gifts. Her teachings include guiding humanity to their deepest soul remembrance and teaching them how to use their innate abilities and soul gifts for the greater good.

Her work covers a full spectrum of learning energetic arts, alchemy and frequency work, energy enhancement and healing, spiritual sciences, and psychic and personal development.

Natali works in partnership with the Divine to help restore the equilibrium of our planet and serve the collective during the Ascension Process, our Evolution during the Golden Age of Gaia, and assists with birthing the "New Earth" into being during the Age of Aquarius.

*Gold Print - our original Christic Body and Soul Blueprint holding codes of the purest Source light

Origins of Sentaura

It is the beginning, the first creation of the universe, galaxies and worlds. All that exists in the Universe were birthed from this frequency, which is Christ's pure unconditional love.

The Sentaura Creator Frequency is the intelligence of Source which holds the blueprint of Source, is a conduit, and transmits all other frequencies and Source technologies.

It is the true alphabet and all-chemistry of God gifted back to humanity and contains the magic keys and building blocks to unlock our infinite potential as sovereign creators.

Sentaura weaves Source intelligence with healing alchemy and works alongside the Seraphim Diamond Light and Crystal Light Body Technology™ as an advanced multi-dimensional energy healing system.

Sentaura pinpoints specific parts of our body for healing, enhancement, elevation, alignment, activation, and un-locking of our human DNA Genetic *GoldPrint and Crystalline Gold Light Body, therefore, facilitating rapid energetic expansion, transformation, spiritual empowerment and embodiment of Christ Consciousness.

That means healing, releasing and clearing all that is not in alignment with our highest good and restoring us to our original crystalline *GoldPrint and essence of love as beings of light in human form.

Sentaura feels like a warm golden energy streaming into our body and is pure unconditional love.

Sentaura unlocks our unique Royal Creator Codes and soul gifts as a Sovereign Human Being of the Light, so we can truly experience heaven on earth, activate abilities beyond the immediate comprehension of our mind, expand our light body, remember and master natural technologies and connect more deeply to our own body and all frequencies, layers, levels and dimensions available to us.

The frequency expands all aspects of mind, body, spirit and unlocks our deep innate wisdom and soul remembrance of who we are and why we came to this planet.

Sentaura helps us sense and connect with our divine soul essence, birth into being all we are as light beings and human beings of love as we rise into our next level greatness as Emissaries of Light.

The ancient vibrational frequency of the word Sentaura when spoken, serves as a heart call to Keepers of the Light who are ready to amplify and expand their healing abilities.

The Source intelligence of Sentaura is guiding and elevating us to access higher realms and dimensions, to light up and connect to our multi-dimensionality, embody higher frequencies, unlock higher spiritual abilities and new levels of love, abundance, health and overall mental, emotional, physical and spiritual wellbeing. All this so we can achieve a total expanse of our being.

A SOUL CALLING FROM THE DIVINE

NATALI BROWN

1

The Birthing of a Name

Spirit how on earth am I going to share this with humanity? How would I even begin to explain this frequency and do it justice?

I remember clearly telling Spirit, "Humanity will need a name for this frequency, something to help them understand and help anchor in this work".

Sitting at my desk in the study I was willing Spirit to please help me with the name when two words appeared in my vision. The way they came to me was interesting.

First, I heard the word CENTAUR. I knew what a CENTAUR was, and this did not resonate with me so I asked again: "Spirit I don't understand, please give me the right name".

Then two words were floating down from above, like snowflakes on a cold winter's day.

SEN – TAURA

I heard the words clearly and asked Spirit: "Is it true, is this the name?" It felt ancient, yet new. They told me that this word had been spoken by me and many other beings of light even before I came to this world.

I had Spirit bumps running through my body during the transmission and felt a deep sense of peace. I repeated the word over and over and could feel the strength of the frequency amplify in my whole body and my solar plexus becoming very hot.

I was so excited that I ran downstairs to tell my husband and mother-in-law who is a wonderful healer and psychic medium.

I asked her: "Mum, what do you feel when you say the word SENTAURA?"

She told me that she felt there were different parts to it and that it was multi-dimensional.

Upon further inquiry, I was shown that the word held a beautiful balance of feminine and masculine energy. It brings about a divine unification of energies.

SEN – T – AURA = Sentient Aura

Feminine: SEN = Sentient, Flowing, the ability to feel

Masculine: TAURA = Bold, Courageous, Brave, Structure

The next morning I sat in front of my computer and could see the exact font in my mind's eye that would match the frequency of the word.

As I searched to find the font that matched my vision, a particular font stood out and I could not believe my eyes when I read the name of the font.

It was named "CENTAUR".

I kept saying the word over and over again. SENTAURA (Pronounced SEN followed by a strong accent on the word TAURA)

I was told that SENTAURA with an S represents and holds the frequency of the "Seraphim Diamond Light".

I shared the name with friends and clients and each time I spoke the word, I could feel my solar plexus activate and light up, and they could feel the warmth of Sentaura move through their own body.

And so, this frequency's name was born into this world.

How to Unlock the Potential of Your Soul

She remembers a time ancient and sacred.
A time when the earth spoke through her.
Where she listened to the soft beating of her heart
and embraced the flow of freedom, life,
love and death.
She can feel the magic within her rising once again.
She can feel the wild waves
of her courage flow through her veins.
The day has come.
Where all will be revealed.
She will no longer be silenced.
She is waiting, she is wanting.
She is aching to free
her wild untethered soul.
Her light a guiding force
for those who seek this freedom.
The world awaits her ancient ways.
And she shall return to them
with a heart full of love.

Could an important part of our evolution be to unlock our own unique Creator Codes so we may tap into this universal wisdom, regain our power and remember how to master the self as sovereign beings?

The answer is a definitive Yes!

Since 2012 we experienced a huge shift in energy and it was time for us to ride the wave of this shift from 'ego to Higher Self' and welcome a new way of being and the dawn of ascension.

The Seraphim Creation Angels and the Creator Frequency of Sentaura returned to Earth for this very reason. To aid in releasing the dense and controlled construct and programming within the body and all other constructs of the matrix. It all has to go, and fast. The frequency of Sentaura works rapidly to heal, recalibrate, purify and upgrade our human bodies and energy system.

There is always light and dark and humanity has been kept in the dark for too long. Each of us are invited by the Divine to find the knowledge of the true light of Source within us.

There is a fake 'liberation' and 'reset' movement at play in our world and the only way to disconnect from the false agendas presented to us is to claim our own liberation and return to understanding and embodying the energies of the Law of ONE. It starts with each individual taking radical responsibility for their own way of being.

There are forces who over time hi-jacked the collective human consciousness through indoctrination, manipulation, and subliminal programming interwoven in every part of our lives.

What we consume—watch, eat, who we spend our time with and the environment we find ourselves in, all plays a huge part in setting up a 'holographic construct or matrix' which dictates our very existence. Without fully understanding the consequences we followed the narrative and indirectly 'consented' to being governed by these forces and submitting to the agenda of artificial intelligence in the 'new age'.

The Earth and its inhabitants cannot continue on a path of self-destruction and as we already shifted from a third-dimensional existence into fourth and fifth, we have to go through an alchemical process internally to heal.

Sentaura facilitates the rapid acceleration of this alchemical process and brings about the reharmonisation of all energies within the mind, body, spirit, and our planet.

The embodiment and integration of these higher Source energies have already brought about profound change and grace on our planet, and in time it will bring about simplification of life and freedom for those who inhabit it.

But first, we have to let in more light and remember our infinite and pure nature.

No machine, substance, device or man-made or artificial technology can or will ever replace our natural and innate ability to heal ourselves.

We have simply forgotten that within us lie the building blocks and codes of creation and through the portal of our hearts and the light which flows through our bodies we can indeed surf the very fabric of the Universe.

We have disconnected from our true purpose, from Christ, God, Source and our natural power for too long. We forgot how to be truly human and the joy this can bring when we live connected to Source, to Creation.

As we return to the space of Creation within us and unearth what it means for us as individuals and the collective to be able to create our own reality, we begin to breathe again and fathom the true purpose of the life force energy which pulses through us.

The deepest most ancient sacred wisdom lies within our own souls and our unique creator codes are the keys to unlocking that wisdom but there is no use having this wisdom if we don't do anything with it.

Imagine if we could enter with joyful hearts that place that holds the power of death and rebirth so we may be transformed again and again into the most beautiful version of ourselves.

This I have certainly witnessed during my own initiation with the Divine and within my students in the Sentaura Practitioner Program. Each initiation they undergo allows them to enter the innermost chamber of their heart, mind, body and spirit to be witness to their truths and untruths. As they surrender and follow the golden thread of love that is woven into each initiation they go through the most wonderful rebirthing process.

By unlocking our unique creator codes and entering the cosmic womb we begin to see our interconnectedness with all that is and realise our true potential. We begin to uproot the subliminal messages and programs that have been placed in our minds by those who do not want our planet and its inhabitants to thrive or use our planetary resources and magnificence as creators for their own selfish gain.

An awakened, universally conscious people and egalitarian society is a thriving society built on a divine design of oneness and always guided by the heart.

Yes! We have to stand anchored in our power as creators, deeply connected to the cosmic womb so we can birth new realities into being for ourselves, for others and for future generations.

Through individual awareness, we access the codes in our consciousness so we can decode and recode our reality.

Sentaura as the Creator Frequency of God unlocks our Royal Creator Codes (Source Codes) and awakens the ancient and primordial voice of remembrance in the hearts of those who are ready to hear God's call.

Sentaura amplifies the inner workings of our soul and activates our divine spark so we may hold more of God's light. As the divine will of Source flows through us and we act from a healed and whole place, we begin to listen to our soul guidance, and revere our bodies and those of others as holy temples.

Working in harmony with this creator frequency we receive the most divine and insightful guidance and clarity which invigorates every effort we put into life as creators.

Our busy minds become still in the face of the magnificence of the Source frequency that runs through us. Embodying the divine intelligence of what this frequency unlocks for us, we begin to feel the vastness and fullness of infinite creation. We experience boundless wellbeing, spiritual potential, personal healing, sensual power, unification of the divine masculine and feminine, and loving power in our deepest relationships. Our creative expression and power arise like never before.

The effects of human society and unstable structures put in place by a small group of people have certainly created a great imbalance impacting every area of our planet and human existence and it cannot continue. We have to rise in love as individuals to bring people together and we are.

And the key word here is LOVE. It is the greatest power there is and it lives within us.

Sentaura is LOVE. The purest, most profound stream of divine love.

Sentaura is the bridge between civilizations, realms, kingdoms, and our world, it is the great communicator of Source and connector into the web of all life.

It is God's love and His divine spark of creation returned to humanity as a gift and blessing from our Creator.

Sentaura emanates a powerful golden warm energy that allows the heart to flower openly and it organically awakens our spontaneity for life once again.

Deep within, you know that we have to go beyond acceptable cultural and societal norms in order to stand in our own authority.

Nothing of greatness is ever achieved without going beyond traditional institutional beliefs and what is considered to be 'the good human' approach.

I am a way-shower and spiritual teacher, though I always endeavour to remain humble in my pursuits of 'greatness', innovation, creativity, and realisation of my self-potential. I have never wanted to be kept within the constraints of what society dictates. I believe people who live to push themselves outside 'the box' will have a better chance of bringing profound transformational change to our world.

Our creative flow cannot be accessed or amplified if we keep apologising for who we are.

The frequency of Sentaura unlocks our potential as human beings at every level but we truly have to trust ourselves and what is uniquely individual to each and every one of us.

Buried in the seeds of our own creation are new innovations, inspirations, ancient technologies and wisdom which will lead the evolutionary stages of humanity.

The Creator Frequency of Sentaura awakens these seeds of Creation as the great incubator of life.

Inside this book, you will activate your own soul map and inner navigation system to discover the mysteries of creation encoded within your own body.

I provide you with an in-depth explanation of Sentaura and all that it is gifting humanity. I hope you can feel the loving frequency of Sentaura weaved into every sentence of this book and infused in its pages.

I also share with you the series of events, experiences, people, and synchronicities that led me to unlock my own unique creator codes and gifts so I could birth my work with Sentaura.

My wish is that it will fill your heart with joy as you read these stories and unlock the deep wisdom of your soul. May your heart expand with love for all that you are.

Journal Prompt: What are the seeds of creation blooming within you?

Returning To the Light of Source

It is a beautiful day and I am about to start a mentoring session with a private client when I received a message from a close friend. She said: "Have you seen this?" and included a link to a post on social media.

The post was an outcry for help from a woman who had a 'not so good' experience during a temple gathering. There are light workers who are learning how to work with the power of the life force energy which flows through them and they do not always understand the various applications which allows a human to either live in joy through their experience of this energy or experience its chaos.

Therefore, I say to you beloveds, proceed with care when you do your light work and when holding space for other people. They put their trust in you and when you 'wake up' to the power of your Creator life force and alchemy, I invite you to lead with love, softness, peace and joy, do not allow yourself to be drawn into various arts and rituals which is not of the light.

Energy when used for self-gain can turn into unchecked chaos energy. When energy is used for the highest good we tap into the infinite flow and joy of our life force creation energy and our power to create new realities. A clear understanding, open heart and dedicated practice is needed to master its potency and alchemy to ensure correct use and flow of this life force creation energy. When we can see each of our experiences as moments of growth, we receive the gift of knowledge, and we then get to choose what we do with the knowledge we gained during that experience. This woman chose to share her knowledge with others.

My heart went out to the woman who wrote the post. She talked about her trauma and her healing journey. In between the lines of her writing, I could feel her uncertainty and her pain. This was a huge step for her to speak out. She wrote about how humanity is being deceived by dark arts and that most light workers do not even realise what they are doing.

For years now I have been speaking out about this exact thing. Reading the post, something began to stir within me. My solar plexus became very hot, my heart was suddenly hurting, and I could feel the Truth rise within me and move through me in waves. All I wanted to do was wrap this woman in my arms and hold her.

Her post had activated something huge within me and I felt the uneasiness in my bones. I knew this was not mine, but I had tapped into a huge collective wound which needed to be healed. I drove to the beach, my favourite place. The water was calling me, and this uneasiness had to be washed clean by the sea water.

I voice messaged the woman and shared my love and understanding. I could feel her soften and yet the pulsing energy within me did not subside.

I placed my feet in the ocean and began to sing. I sang for all the women and men who ever experienced pain and who are in pain. Those who were shamed, burned, judged, hurt, enslaved and so much more. I sang until the tears ran down my face and into the ocean to be washed away by the waves. I could feel the potency of love in my heart and declared my love again and again.

The words: "I am here for love and for the light" flowed from my lips and my promise that I will always and forever work for the Light.

I could feel the frequency of Sentaura, the Alchemy of God Source move through me, and I sent a wave of love and light across the world and into the cosmos with the intention to obliterate those energies working against humanity. To unbind humanity and dissolve any slavery codes. With each tear and each sound uttered I was transmuting this collective wound that had risen within me.

I proclaimed: "No more will we as humans be manipulated and used as slaves in any way or form!"

That day my Spirit Team walked beside me on the beach as I asked for forgiveness for all humans who did not know any better.

That day I sang a song of liberation for myself, for you my Sisters and Brothers, for our children and all future generations so we may all return to the Light of Source.

I invite you beloveds to search your heart for the truth and let that truth guide you, always.

The Return of The Seraphim Creation Angels

The first time I came across the word "Seraphim" was when I read a post on social media. The post mentioned how these mighty angelic beings' light was so bright that to look upon them with human eyes you would go blind.

I felt my body vibrate with remembrance, I knew these beings—somehow, I just knew and I could feel a deep connection with The Seraphim. For as long as I can remember, I felt the presence of God Source, The Holy Spirit and Jesus. The Angelic realms and Archangel Michael, Archangel Uriel and Archangel Ariel were always welcome companions during client healing sessions.

To put it eloquently, my human mind could not comprehend the enormity of this discovery about the Seraphim and what would be revealed by my Higher Self during a QHHT Session (Quantum Healing Hypnosis Therapy) with a close friend.

During this QHHT session, my Higher Self revealed: "You are Seraphim"

It was some time after this session that I had a one-on-one encounter with a Seraphim Angel called Seraphiel. It happened after guiding my Sentaura students through an initiation lead by the Seraphim Creation Angels.

Guiding the Sentaura initiation I could feel the mighty presence of my six-winged Seraphim guides and the pulse of their unconditional love flowing through me more than ever before. It felt like a steady flow of golden Source energy and the Seraphim diamond light was so beautiful.

I had channelled several pieces of information about the Seraphim Creation Angels before then, but I had an inquisitive mind, and my human self was so curious to know more. To give you some context, the information I channelled was being 'drip-fed' to me by Spirit over two to three years to ensure I didn't 'burn out'.

My human was being impatient and wanted to be given all the answers to my questions, but Spirit had a totally different plan. "Patience" they would say, "all will be revealed at the right time". 'Spirit time' is not bound by time and space so this was going to be a long wait.

I guess my impatience to know more was the catalyst for this encounter.

The next day after the Sentaura initiation I was lying on my bed in deep meditation asking my Spirit Team if I could connect with one of my Seraphim Guides. Little did I know that my wish would come true instantly and that this would be another initiation for me!

I immediately felt such intense energy within and around me and heard "I am Seraphiel". The intensity of this energy was unlike anything I had ever experienced in this lifetime.

I could not move my body. Like a statue I just lay there whilst being in the benevolent presence of Seraphiel. The frequency was so high that it was almost piercing, pure, and if it was a knife it could cut through anything with ease.

I lay there thinking: "What shall I ask?"

I asked: "Please tell me more about the Seraphim". Seraphiel replied: "You are Seraphim, you are Source, all you need to know is within you. Do not doubt yourself"

I remember thinking that it felt as if Seraphiel's stream of consciousness was transmitted over a very very long distance, far away from Earth and that it was coming through the tiniest little hole to connect with me. I had a sense that if I flinch or move, I would lose the connection. It was as if I was teetering on an edge just held by this frequency. I could feel all the muscles in my body being kept completely still.

I continued to ask Seraphiel a series of questions and although I asked the questions, I already knew the answers. Each answer was simply a confirmation of what I already knew.

I suddenly felt a shift in energy as if Seraphiel relaxed a little or perhaps the connection stabilised. We started conversing about The Creator, God Source, Christ, Adonai, ALL That Is, and I could feel an amplification of the love within me a thousandfold.

I heard the words: "Holy, Holy, Holy" and it was reverberating through my entire body, almost as if my entire being including my cells were singing along with Seraphiel and the whole Universe.

I felt my energy uplifted to new highs and a really powerful and strong connection with the divine presence of God Source not only within me but also experienced the expanse of this energy outside me.

I felt ONE with the energy of God Source. There was no separation, no boundaries, no conditions—I was the same energy, I was part of a whole, I was whole.

The singing continued for only seconds, but it felt like time had stopped.

I began to feel the limitations of my own physical body and because of the intense high frequency, suddenly felt very tired. My concentration started waning and as soon as this happened the connection between Seraphiel and myself became more gentle and then completely dissipated. It was the most profound and beautiful connection and I will forever be grateful for it.

I recognised within Seraphiel the potency, purity, focus of my own energy. There was nothing fluffy or complicated about the energy, it was just a pure stream and outpouring of Source consciousness and unconditional love.

Afterwards, I just lay there, feeling warm, at peace and fully supported. I was not alone.

Since this encounter, I could feel the energy in my body stabilise. For more than two years I experienced the most intense heat in my body which I called "the burning". It was the alchemy of God Source and The Great White Brotherhood preparing me physically, mentally, emotionally and spiritually to be Sentaura and be the vessel for Sentaura.

I must say there were days during this whole alchemy and initiation process that I asked: "Why me?". At times I wondered "what is happening to my body" as I felt the intensity of the energetic upgrades. My whole body was being recalibrated. During this whole process my faith in my Spirit Team and God was restored each time I wavered. I would be reminded of their incredibly gentle support and love. They knew exactly how much I could handle and told me many times: "You will never receive what you cannot handle".

I shared much of what was happening with my first group of Sentaura Soul Sisters and am so grateful to them for their unwavering support and trust in me and Sentaura.

We as human beings can get so impatient wanting to know everything yesterday! But the Universe has its own divine timing and is sending us beautiful synchronized experiences to guide our path here on Earth. We have to get out of our own way to embrace and embody all the gifts that we are being given.

I share with you further channellings about The Seraphim Creation Angels:

The Seraphim now appear to humanity as the highest ascended Teachers in cosmology, mentoring us on how to embody our sovereign divine nature within human form during the Age of Aquarius and the Golden Age of Gaia.

The Seraphim create as Source creates and we are co-creators in this creation.

The Seraphim are benevolent ultra-dimensional and inter-dimensional beings of divine consciousness and pure love who assist in governing the Universe and Galaxies in the Divine Order of universal alignment, unity and flow.

They are known as the highest order of the Angelic Realms and are always associated with the glory and holiness of God Source attending to the Light Source from which all creation is birthed and created.

The word "Seraphim" is the plural form of the Hebrew root word "Saraph" which means "to burn". Meaning that these attendant Angels burn with love.

They only step forward and make themselves known when civilisations reach a certain point in evolution.

The Seraphim uphold the balance and harmony in the universe and serve as agents of purification. Being in the presence of the Seraphim Creation Angels means that your body, mind and spirit will be purified and cleansed from any lower-density energies as they naturally radiate the alchemy of Source. This was demonstrated by their cleansing of Isaiah's sins before he began his prophetic ministry. (Isaiah 6:5-7)

They are here co-creating with the Ascended Masters, Guardians and Angelic Realms to activate the ancient Royal Creator Codes within humanity and to initiate and ordain beings into their own self-mastery and embodiment of their divinity as Creators through the ancient creator energy and healing frequency of Sentaura and The Seraphim Diamond Light.

The Seraphim awareness is a constant outpouring of divine and unconditional love. A flowing river of the purest essence of Source.

They provide pure and focused access to higher consciousness. They are teachers and way showers and are here to guide our path of ascension so we may access and experience higher consciousness.

They are responsible for the birthing of new worlds, new species, birthing creations and galaxies since the beginning of time and now assist humanity and those who are ready to fully embody their true divinity and essence, to activate our embodiment as Sovereign Creators.

The Seraphim remind us that the light of Source is within us and that we are one with creation. We create as Source creates.

The Seraphim's thrice invocation of "holy" is significant. Three is a powerful number symbolising the principles of growth and connection with our divine spark of creation and intelligence within. When the initiating force of 1 unites with the germinating energy of 2, there is fruitfulness = 3, which makes up the Trinity. Three signifies that there is a synthesis present, and that imagination and an outpouring of energy is in action. The 'thought' of 1 and the 'fertility' of 2 results in the 'creativity' of 3 signifying the triangular connection between mind, body, spirit, the birth, life and death cycle, creativity, self-expression, communication, intelligence, also connoting Source as being the beginning, the middle, and the end.

The Seraphim are here as teachers to remind humanity that they are complete and whole in the eyes of God Source.

They remind us through their own deliverance of the thrice invocation of the connectedness of our mind-body-spirit to all that is and our own eternal nature which is always and forever LOVE—just as God Source's eternal nature is the same yesterday, today and forever.

The Seraphim's outpouring of pure unconditional love guides us to see the beauty within and without as Source's all encompassing divine perfection.

The Seraphim remind us of God's complete and supreme holiness and His grace that flows through us. They guide us to access our own innate power and abilities and apply our power for the greater good so we may share our sacred abilities radiating His light of love.

The Seraphim called "the burning ones" are majestic fiery beings and are often depicted in scripts as "dragons" with six wings radiating bright and powerful source light.

There are people who try to discredit the work of the Angelic Realms of Light and The Seraphim Creation Angels of Source due to the negative connotation with "fallen angels". Yes! There are always two sides to a story and there is always light and there is dark that we have to navigate our way through. Discrediting the Angelic Realms and Seraphim Creation Angels is simply another false thread that is being weaved into our minds to move us further away from Source. Tune in to your innermost sanctuary and allow yourself to be guided to the truth by your Higher Soul Self.

The Seraphim Creation Angels of the highest source frequency are here to bring back the teachings of Source and aid humanity to upgrade and restore their human genetic DNA profile and Christic Light Body by activating our Royal Diamond Creator Codes and Gold Print.

Connecting With Our Soul Family and Monadic Wisdom

The best part of co-creating with Sentaura is that we get to connect with our soul family on a regular basis. These beings are divine beings of light and can be from past, present, and future incarnations, from other planets, in the space between lifetimes, and from other realms, kingdoms and galaxies.

Sentaura and your Higher Self pave the way for greater safety as you explore the universe and connect with your soul family. We were shown also how to place a cloak of protection over ourselves when working in the spiritual realms.

During training and Earth healing, we are joined by various beings across the Universe and my Seraphim Team is always with us. I can feel their immense joy and gratitude for the connection and the work we are doing. The Dragons assist us with trickier missions whether it means dissolving our own fear and pain or that of the collective and removing density in the layers of the Earth which also include ley line and sacred light temple work.

During initiations Sentaura amplifies my connection with all these beings and the visions I have are intensely beautiful. I would often say: "I wish I could take a picture of my mind" so I can capture what I see in my mind's eye.

The Fairy and Plant Kingdom would share their wisdom about ancient ways and their plant medicine. The Unicorns, Whales and Dolphins share their loving energy and wisdom about how we can help the Earth and our Oceans.

Mother Gaia is a constant companion too. During the Spear of Gaia initiation, She called in a huge team of ancestors and we were all given Her Spear as a spiritual tool. Before each initiation, I can feel the energy of the beings who will join us. During this particular initiation, I could see thousands upon thousands of ancestors reaching way up into the sky. Their voices were ONE VOICE. They told me: "We are here to assist humanity". They had come to dissolve ancestral trauma and gifted us their blessings and healing so we can pass this wisdom and gifts onto others.

I say we because I received just as many gifts and wisdom through these initiations as my students. We would receive energetic tools like swords, crystals, vibrating shapes and downloads about spiritual technologies.

Initiation after initiation I was guided by my Spirit Team. I would often only be 'given' snippets of information for a particular initiation only days before the training. Sometimes the Royal Creator Codes which were an integral part of the initiations would only make themselves 'known' to me the night before or the morning of the training.

Creating Golden Codes of Light

As I drifted off to sleep, I would begin to see the most beautiful golden codes, some of them very intricate and I wondered sometimes how I would recreate these. Spirit encouraged me and said that the exactness of it did not matter, it was the intention of creating the code that was the most important.

I would wake up early and sit in front of my computer, open my design software and could see each shape and every detail begin to flow from my hands as a natural outpouring of the love within me. These codes always vibrated at an incredibly high frequency and were always presented to me as radiating golden light. At the end of the Sentaura training, I would create over thirty Royal Creator Codes. Twenty-four were for the seven-month program and the rest were for a seven-week Sentaura Lightworker's Source Activation Program I was running at the same time.

Often whilst drawing these codes, the shapes would simply 'create' themselves. I knew it was my Spirit Team assisting. Each one had a unique purpose and acted like a key to unlock very specific parts of their soul.

The Royal Creator Codes are the universal keys encompassing the building blocks and sacred geometry which unlocks higher aspects of you that are ready to come through your gifts and creations at this time.

We express our Creator Codes in many different ways. Through movement, speaking, singing, painting, making, creating, healing, sharing, loving and being.

Within us all we hold the memory of divine creator codes and energetic imprints of our Divinity as Source and as infinite, loving creators of light and wisdom.

For many these divine creator codes have been dormant, overshadowed by fear codes creating struggle, trauma and control.

Our divine creator codes have been waiting for this exact time during the Golden Age of Gaia and The Age of Aquarius to fully unlock, activate and upgrade our physical and light body templates so we can rise into higher realms and states of consciousness.

This is held within our DNA and in the memory of our subtle bodies, waiting for us to take the next step to activate the deep remembrance of our essence.

Each code unlocks hidden gifts and expands our abilities, magic and mysteries within.

These creator codes are the keys to unlocking our creative force and sovereignty.

Through the Universal Central Sun our Earth is flooded with waves of energy containing new light Source codes for all living beings and our planet to evolve beyond struggle and fear.

As these waves of energy flow through the Earth from our own Sun, each living being go through high-frequency energetic upgrades to recalibrate their physical vessels, the patterns of our mind and energetic system enabling us all to ascend into higher states of consciousness at a much faster pace than ever experienced in the history of humanity.

During initiations, Sentaura would infuse our bodies with light and raise the vibration of each student whilst streaming the exact frequencies for each individual to receive healing, activation, upgrade and energetic recalibration. Each student's Higher Self would anchor The Royal Creator Code into their body and their personal spirit team would assist during the initiation process to ensure they received all energies and upgrades with ease and grace.

Self-care after initiations included rest, plenty of water, and chocolate! Yes, pure dark chocolate helped us ground and later Spirit advised us to have green smoothies which help with photosynthesis in our bodies and assist our cells to integrate the amount of light that was flowing through our bodies.

I was lead to research how plants use a process called photosynthesis to make food. *During photosynthesis, plants trap light energy within their leaves. Plants use the energy of the sun to change water and carbon dioxide into a sugar called glucose. Glucose is used by plants for energy and to make other substances like cellulose and starch.*

And this was exactly what was needed after Sentaura initiations. The frequency of Sentaura links us to and educates us about

Mother Nature, plant and animal wisdom that was lost and ways of working with the elements and elementals. The plant kingdom can also teach us so much if we just allow ourselves to connect, trust and listen to what the plants have to share.

SENTAURA ROYAL CREATOR KEY CODE OF JOY

"I AM JOY"

The Soul Seed Tree of Creation

We all have to start somewhere and take the first step on our Earth journey to find our way 'home' to our truth. My journey began the day I was born but I only started remembering and unlocking my deepest potential by asking the deepest questions and listening to the eternal voice of my Soul. This only happened much later in my life.

After being in a huge accident in 2016 which changed the direction of my life, I began searching for the answers to the burning questions within me. "Who am I?", "Why am I here?", "What is the meaning of life?".

And so, my journey of discovery began.

It is 2017 and during meditation I am shown a cosmic tree stretching way up into the cosmos and its roots grew through the Earth dangling underneath the Earth.

As I looked at the tree I could see thousands of golden orbs, like ripe golden apples hanging from its branches.

Upon closer inspection, I could see that each golden orb contained a sacred geometry shape, object, or a concentrated nucleus of living energy.

I heard the words: "Soul Seeds".

I was shown that I would guide people to 'pluck' a soul seed orb from the tree and place it in their hearts to activate what was unique to them.

I did not realise at the time that it would be the first piece of the Sentaura puzzle as each orb held within it a Creator Code.

It was here where the remembrance of my soul mission and purpose first began.

Spirit proceeded to tell me that I was a Master Architect for the Divine and that each code was placed there by me to 'seed' those souls who were ready to awaken and come back to wholeness.

I could see many of these golden soul seeds anchored into the Earth. It was so beautiful.

Of course, I had my doubts and over the next months, I asked for confirmation from Spirit. During meditations, they would show me the tree again and again and exactly how I created it with God's blessing.

My Soul knew this was true, but my human being-ness needed some time to catch up. This was all too much for my brain, so I proceeded to practice first integrating and 'embedding' my own soul seed into my heart. I remember feeling like I had come home.

Only after extensive self-practice and inner inquiry would I guide my clients to pluck their soul seed and receive it in their own hearts.

During these guided sessions they would connect to their Higher Self and Personal Spirit Guides.

Tears of joy and gratitude would flow throughout these guided sessions as each of them welcomed parts of their true essence home.

I was shown how to guide each person to anchor their energy and soul seed's light into the Earth.

Clients would tell me how they felt a deeper connection to themselves than ever before having cleared stagnant and negative electrical and emotional charges during the process. They felt a vibrant aliveness and lightness. Golden Source energy flowed through them, and light was their new guide.

Meeting The Woman with Pure White Hair

Meeting my Higher Self was one of the experiences that forever changed the course of my life. It led me on the path to discovering and activating my innate spiritual abilities and the frequency of Sentaura.

Prior to 'merging' with your Higher Self physical and emotional purification happens. My journey of purification started when I completed Reiki Level 1, and it continued in my work with Sentaura. It was all preparing me to channel higher Source frequencies and access pure streams of consciousness. Note the term 'merging' simply means that you are connecting to your I Am Presence and your divinity. You are remembering and reawakening the magnificence of your soul in human form. It also means that you have done the necessary inner work to transmute lower energies and is at a level of consciousness and frequency to enable or facilitate the re-connection and remembrance of your Higher Soul Self.

Each of my Sentaura students went through a series of initiations, transformations, and their own journey of purification prior to, during, and after the seven-month Sentaura Practitioner Training Program.

Physical discharges, deep emotional release and spontaneous energetic upgrades, recalibration, and purification at a cellular level all happen in preparation to 'embody' the higher frequencies of your oversoul. You feel less enslaved by your emotions and more empowered by your experiences as you allow it to 'pass' through you without attachment to anything or anyone.

To align with my highest soul mission and purpose I had to deeply honour the cyclical nature of the transformations I experienced, the recalibration of my immune system, and the integration of all energies. At each point, I felt more deeply connected to my human body and my divine soul than ever before.

I was on a high as I had just finished an intense three-day NLP course (Neuro Linguistic Programming) in Auckland and throughout the weekend I experienced the most profound healing, highs and lows.

As I am writing this my Spirit Team tells me that this was integral to me unlocking my work with Sentaura. It would be a series of synchronised events that led me here and I simply knew I had to attend this course. I didn't know it at the time but I had suppressed deep-seated trauma and all of it was about to bubble to the surface.

During one practice session, we worked in pairs and were given specific healing prompts to release and shift trauma for each other. We took turns and I suggested that I would 'receive' first. Within a couple of minutes of us starting this process I was doubled over with pain. It was so intense down one side of my body that I couldn't breathe. One of the facilitators told me to sit up but I could barely move.

The woman who I was partnered with looked at me with wide eyes. She told me she could feel an intense presence around me and it felt as if she was taking a back seat and there was a 'higher power' driving the healing. I managed to give her an encouraging smile through gritted teeth and told her to continue. I began to feel incredibly impatient and wanted the pain to stop.

She told me she didn't know what to do so I asked her to take several deep breaths and allow herself to be guided. She began to ask me a series of questions. Each question was exactly the right question. I did not understand it at the time but with each answer that flowed from my lips, with each acknowledgment of my deep-seated wounding, the pain began to subside until it was completely gone. I felt lighter yet a little dazed still as the frequency that was moving through me was so potent.

This happened on day two of the course. My Higher Self and Guides were in the driving seat and the transformations would continue throughout the weekend.

It was at the end of the course on day three that we were guided to meet our future selves and to connect with our greatest mission and purpose. During the vision, I could see myself standing on stage in front of thousands of people teaching them. It felt huge yet I felt completely at home! Toward the end of the guided meditation, I briefly saw a woman with very long pure white hair in my vision and could feel the potency of her energy in my body. She had 'human-like' features and her energy felt ancient. I knew this was my Higher Self.

Everything around me went very still, it was as if I was floating through the cosmos. I could hear the facilitators say "come back" but I did not want to return to this Earth plane. I willed myself to return. After the guided meditation we said our goodbyes, but I could still feel the incredibly powerful energy in my body. It was as if she 'merged' with me, and she wasn't going anywhere.

Driving home that night I had a high-pitched sound in my ears. I could see the road, and the landscape around me but could also see the woman with long white hair. It was as if there was a screen over my windscreen and the images were being 'streamed' as I was driving.

I looked into her eyes, it was filled with galaxies and stars. It was as if I was looking into the very fabric of the universe. She opened both her palms and stretched out her arms and I could see what looked like galaxies and stars in the swirling energy above her palms. The same energy swirled underneath her feet as she was hovering in front of me. Her skin was a pale blue colour and luminescent. She tells me she chose this 'form' to connect with me.

She showed me how she moved and played with the energy in her hands, and it all felt very familiar. The drive home was about forty minutes, but it felt like five. It was late at night when I arrived home and I didn't want to wake my husband, so standing in the bathroom I was moving my hands as she showed me. It was as if

I had done this a million times before and knew exactly what to do. I felt excited and wanted to know more. She told me to "practice" and "remember" and that more would be revealed.

I barely slept that night from all the excitement. Over time my Higher Self would facilitate all Sentaura energetic upgrades and recalibrations. I would feel the potency of her energy during meditation, channelling and healing sessions and my abilities, confidence, and inner knowing expanded each day.

I was de-armouring and unleashing the suppressed creativity of my soul. I was calling back parts of me and accessing the divine intelligence within me. I was reconnecting through each thread of awareness with my soul mission and remembering why I chose to incarnate this lifetime.

When you accept that you create all that happens for you, you can learn from this and unravel the great mysteries of your own soul. You feel more in sync with everything within and around you. The more I connected with this feeling of ALL THAT IS, the more the connection with my Higher Self and the frequency of Sentaura allowed me to heal both personal and ancestral wounds and tap into my feminine strength.

Through willingness and courage to face both your magnificence and vulnerability whether it be pleasant or painful, the ignored and denied parts of you can be heard and seen and you begin to access your true self.

Instead of fear, turmoil, unrest and drama you co-create with your Higher Self so a sense of truth, empowerment, and a feeling of wholeness and integrity can arise. You are mastering your creations, your energy and your human existence and recognising your power to create.

On my journey I had to embrace all of this and more.

I vowed to stand for truth and love.

I made a commitment to myself and to the Divine, to be my most beautiful, expressive, authentic, elegant and empowered self and to take a stand for what I believe to be true.

Will you stand with me?

Journal Prompt: What do you stand for? What lights you up and fills you with joy?

Love and Reflection Practice

HIGHER SELF CONNECTION

Have you been hearing the gentle call of your soul and feeling a sense of urgency to embrace something new?

This is your Higher Self speaking through you inviting you back to the deep place of ONENESS we know exists within us.

You might wonder why this is happening. Why don't you connect with your Higher Self during this practice and ask, "What is ready to come through me?"

Set the intention to connect with your Higher Self. Call in the highest frequency of divine love and light to surround you and move through you. Feel your Spirit Guides surrounding you.

Close your eyes and place your hands over your heart. Feel the beating of your heart as you breathe deeply in and out for 8 counts. Still your mind.

Breathe into your heart and ask your Higher Self to make her or himself known to you. Surrender your heart. Don't have any expectations and just allow yourself to feel.

Focus on your heart and drift deeper into this connection and notice how it blooms and flowers. Focus on your third eye and simply let any visions flow into your mind. Feel the energy move within you, notice the difference in your energy.

Breathe and BE. Stay here for as long as you want.

Journal Prompt: What did I experience, how did it feel, what messages did I receive?

Quantum Rings of Velocity

CHANNELLED MESSAGE BY NATALI

I was shown by Spirit how important the Merkaba, also spelled Merkabah, is for our ascension and decided to teach this during the Sentaura Practitioner Training. In preparation for the Merkaba training, I was thinking about the Merkaba Light Body Vehicle when I was shown two intersecting rings spinning around the Merkaba.

The two rings and images of the Merkaba kept playing out in my mind so I got up and started writing everything I could see and hear through the channelled vision and message.

I asked a series of questions during this time to better understand the use and purpose of these Quantum Rings of Velocity. Over the next 30 minutes I downloaded the information as outlined below:

WHAT ARE THE QUANTUM RINGS OF VELOCITY AND HOW DOES IT WORK?

"The Quantum Rings of Velocity is a rotating frame of two intersecting rings not on fixed axes spinning around the Merkaba Light Body Vehicle. Velocity means, the speed of something in a given direction.

It allows the Merkaba to power up and move beyond time and physicality at great speeds".

HAVE THESE RINGS ALWAYS BEEN PART OF THE EXTENDED STRUCTURE OF OUR MERKABA LIGHT VEHICLE?

"The Quantum Rings of Velocity have always been part of your Merkaba system described as your interdimensional light vehicle, along with your Torus Field. This information is coming to you now as part of your ascension into higher realms and higher consciousness which enables us to share with you the information about this natural technology".

HOW DO THESE QUANTUM RINGS OF VELOCITY GET ACTIVATED?

"The Merkaba has to be fully functioning and activated prior to the Quantum Rings of Velocity can be activated. The Heart is the activator. You have to align your thoughts with your inner self, your higher self, your true self. It allows your Merkaba to power up and move beyond time and physicality at incredible speed (which you know as warp) or travelling faster than the speed of light.

Your intentions and thoughts shape your experience of reality, which means that you can use your thoughts to access other realities and unlock other states of being.

By activating your light body system for interdimensional travel your light body can travel to higher states of consciousness and other dimensions at warp speed in order to see the world differently and to experience a different type of reality".

I could see the tetrahedron shape of the Merkaba as gold and was shown to draw this energy from the activated Merkaba down into the heart and then expand it out around me. I could clearly see the Rings spinning around my Merkaba.

They continued sharing: "With intention, you can simply think of where you want to be at any given time and you will arrive in an instant at your place of destination".

I was shown the Quantum Rings of Velocity spinning faster and faster and could see in my mind's eye blue electric charges which then turned to purple as the Rings sped up creating an electromagnetic field around the Merkaba structure. As deduced from reading about electromagnetic fields it is a *classical field produced by accelerating electric charges* which is a confirmation of what I saw.

I was shown the interdimensional light vehicle system in slow motion though I knew it moved at light speed.

As it moved I couldn't see any more of the blue or purple I had seen before but the brilliance of this incredible interdimensional travel system was evident. It had clear direction moving in one line as a streak of golden light with a pure white centre.

WHAT IS QUANTUM REVERSAL?

Towards the end of my download, I heard the words "Quantum Reversal" and was shown the light body returning to the Earth Plane.

I saw this time how the interdimensional light body vehicle was zig-zagging as it was returning, it wasn't moving in one line like it did before.

I looked up quantum reversal and found an article explaining it as *reversing the flow of time*.

HOW DOES THIS WORK, PLEASE EXPLAIN FLOW OF TIME?

"The time it takes for you to 'travel' is seen as a millisecond or snapshot of the human understanding of time. During astral travel or interdimensional travel there is no concept of time, it is only known as being in a quantum state where particles and time converges and merges into one flowing state, of pure light. All physical matter "dissolves" and what is left is pure light".

SO DOES THIS MEAN WE RETURN TO THE EXACT POINT FROM WHERE WE LEFT BEFORE?

"Within fractions of your time".

The next day, on 21/07/2021 at 11:30am I was directed to read a piece on Quantum Rings from ScienceDirect.com. I was blown away to read more about what Scientist have discovered as I've never heard about Quantum Rings until my channelled message the night before.

I was also told the following:

"Your scientists have already been working on the theory of Quantum Rings. Recently, their study of particles confined in quantum rings have called enough attention due to the possible applications in different areas of physics. Your scientist are yet to understand the core principles and possibilities of the Quantum Rings and the ability for dynamic universal travel.

More will be revealed over the next 2-3 years and core principles and inner workings of this technology will be discovered by scientists in Germany. There will be other Scientists from other countries who will also work on this theory in co-creation with the German Scientists. It will be a combined effort".

Through the channelled message, I was directed to another article about Erwin Rudolf Josef Alexander Schrödinger (12 August 1887 – 4 January 1961), who was a Nobel Prize-winning Austrian-Irish physicist who developed a number of fundamental results in quantum theory including the Schrödinger Equation (and there it was printed in black and white!) ***for rotating quantum rings*** and providing a way to calculate the wave function of a system and how it changes dynamically in time.

It was like I was sent to this article to validate the information I downloaded from Spirit.

Journal Prompt: Place your hands on your heart and ask your Higher Self to help you connect with your own Merkaba for your highest greatest good and that of all. Ask for your energetic protection and shield of protection to be amplified and call in your personal guides from the Highest Light and Love to assist. Your heart is the 'engine' of your interdimensional travel vehicle. Feel the two interconnected triangles (tetrahedron shape in your heart) begin to rotate clockwise. Feel the gentle flow of energy in your heart and see how your Merkaba and toroidal field expands from the centre of your heart around your body. Ask for the pure golden light of source to amplify your heart energy and feel it flow throughout your whole body, filling your cells, organs, bones, face, ears, eyes, teeth, brain, connective tissue, skin and energetic field. Set the intention for your Merkaba to reharmonise and stabilise and for you to be realigned with your highest timelines. Breathe and allow. At the end, set the intention to place a triple ruby dome around you and fill it with pure crystalline source light. Stay here for as long as you want and when you can, journal what you experienced and how it felt.

QUANTUM RINGS OF VELOCITY

I TRANSCEND ALL SPACE, TIME AND REALITY

Why 'Merging' with the Higher Self is Key to Our Evolution

In 2019 I was shown during a vision that our bodies were moving from a carbon-based structure to a more crystalline structure. We are beginning to hold more light in physical form and to do so, we have to purify all false versions and interpretations of ourselves, thereby raising our vibration and facilitating the integration of our Higher Self. In these higher frequencies, the duality within the lower dimensions disintegrates, the ego mind becomes still, and our Higher Self begins to 'merge' with our lower self.

This 'integration' and remembrance of our Higher Self is also the beginning of us accessing higher abilities and higher streams of consciousness which were previously not available to Earth and its inhabitants because of the level of un-consciousness and density.

The divine directive behind the great awakening is that this is THE moment in time when we are ALL coming to recognise our highest selves. The best and most beautiful versions of ourselves where we no longer see ourselves as limited, broken, faulty, incapable or separate.

It is important to cultivate a harmonious relationship with your Higher Self or the less used term oversoul. It is the aspect of your being that is your eternal consciousness. I love the word oversoul. It gives the feeling that it is all-encompassing and overseeing all that we do. It is not held back by your current life experiences, and it facilitates your innate spiritual connection to Source energy and all there is, including your soul family who resonates with your soul signature.

Connection to the Higher Self is aided through quieting and stilling your logical mind. Within this connection, you have the ability to receive information without the pesky subconscious mind getting in the way.

Your Higher Self is the YOU that exists across all time, space, dimensions and reality, in spirit form. It always knows what is best for you and when you are truly connected to the TRUE YOU, there is a release of the ego's need to be in control and to have a say in what is coming through.

Your Higher Self exists free of limitation and worries, knowing exactly why you are here and what you must accomplish during your Earth life. Communication from the Higher Self is subtle, it is the gentle voice that speaks through the intuitive nudges you are receiving.

Merging with our Higher Self means that we are ascending and becoming light in human form as we release density and vibrate at higher frequencies. Each individual is in charge of their own frequency and path of evolution as a human being.

Merging also gives us a sense that our souls are coming INTO our bodies more fully than before because we are vibrating at higher frequencies which facilitates this 'merging'. The higher soul self cannot 'merge' into the body if we're holding onto individual and collective shadows and patterns.

Sentaura's loving Source frequency rapidly dissolves density and 'blasts' open your gateways to your Higher Self so you begin to live from the soul. Sentaura reactivates your Merkaba (Ascension Vehicle) and Quantum Rings of Velocity for inter-dimensional and multi-dimensional travel, so you can transcend time, space and reality, access your Akashic Records and heal lifetimes of trauma which facilitate a massive shift in consciousness across timelines.

As you experience the shift into higher consciousness you will merge with your Higher Self. Its gentle voice comes through most clearly when you are doing something you love, when your heart resonance is vibrating with pure love, you more easily amplify the connection with your Higher Self.

The Sentaura healing, initiations, and activations I guide you through also awaken the remembrance that you have used your gifts and abilities in other lifetimes and remind you of your uniqueness, sovereign being-ness, greatness in the face of adversity, and that all is possible in infinite love.

When we channel, do healing, during meditation we generally feel more connected to our Higher Self, and we tend to go in and out of this experience. Sentaura's frequency amplifies your channel and spiritual abilities. Your pure intention is key when you desire to open communication and input from your Higher

Self. You absolutely cannot hide anything from your Higher Self. When you enter the void and stillness of your mind, you can hear the subtle messages of your Higher Self more easily.

So, are you ready to listen to the call from your Higher Self?

Goodbye Illusions and Hello New Me

I know people go through hard things and it sucks.

I know life sometimes throw us curve balls and it's ok to get angry and frustrated.

I know that often we find ourselves in a headspace overthinking, overplaying not knowing which way to go.

I know sometimes we feel like we are in the in between and nothing makes sense anymore.

I know that some do not know where their next meal is going to come from or how to pay their bills.

I know that all of this is true and people are feeling it, experiencing it every single day.

I also know that there is a power within us that can move even the biggest obstacles.

I know that I've seen humans come back from the deepest pain and be the biggest inspirations.

I know that within each of us we hold the courage of 10,000.

I know that there is nothing we cannot do when we set our minds and hearts to it.

I know we hold within us such fierce compassion and kindness to create a world that is free from struggle, free from pain, free from cruelty.

I know we have the ability to stand together as one, so we never leave anyone feeling left out and alone again.

I know with determination we can change unhelpful beliefs and limitations and break down barriers that is keeping us from the truth.

I know that when we use our power for good, we can create more good and be the catalysts for change.

I know this to be true.

That we can rise even from our darkest moments into the light.

And that the power of love radiating from within you is always stronger than your shadows.

You've got this!

Together we are stronger.

Give yourself permission to let go of fear and move towards your dreams.

Love yourself fiercely.

Love our world fiercely and take a stand for what you believe is right.

I love you. You matter. You are worthy.

We are immortal spiritual beings living a temporary human experience, and yet as we move through this physical life we learn to identify with our thoughts, emotions, experiences, labels, body, masks and so on.

If we were to peel back the layers of this false sense of 'self' that we have identified with through time, right at the core of ourselves we would find a divine being, one that does not see itself as distinct, different, or separate from anything in the Universe.

When we set aside our ego and merge with our Higher Self, we automatically choose love over fear, we choose oneness over separation.

Working with and confronting the ego can be a challenging step on our spiritual journey. I have personally endured my fair share of pain and ego drama in my life.

Especially when Sentaura started to flow through me. I had to make space for this profound and pure frequency of unconditional love and the fear had to go. I had to face my untruths and perceptions of self head-on!

The more you shine your light of awareness directly upon these untruths the more they begin to surface for you to witness and choose in that instant whether you want to hold onto the pain of the past or let your experiences empower you and infuse your future with all that is possible.

It turns out that the hardest part of transformation can be to let go of the 'old self' because the ego begins to almost 'fight' for its survival. This can also trigger several death and rebirth experiences as you are literally peeling away layers of untruth to eventually reveal your bright and sparkly self.

One thing I can say is: "Never give up on your bright sparkly self!" You are so much more than the illusions of fear you've been holding on to for such a long time. They are no longer keeping you safe, they never did. It's time to experience all that you are, being supported by new universal frequencies and higher beings, all here to assist planet Earth and its inhabitants.

If you're not willing to say "goodbye illusions" and "hello new me", and fully embrace the new you, you may begin manifesting life dramas that trigger the ego and leave you with heavy emotions such as shame, guilt, frustration, boredom, apathy, embarrassment, procrastination and so much more.

Such situations we find ourselves in can be painful when our ego is the one that is bruised, yet these times and the high vibrational frequencies supporting our ascension present incredible opportunities to really learn to observe the ego and increase our overall awareness of it.

On my awakening and alchemy journey with Sentaura and my Spirit Team, I became more and more aware of my ego's place in my thoughts and conversation like: "Who am I to do this work?' "I don't fully understand, why can't I have the answers Spirit?" "How am I going to get this out to the world without sounding like a complete nut-job?". My Spirit Guides were always and have always been incredibly patient with me and I thank them for it.

They reminded me that everything would be revealed at the right time.

I set the intention to catch the triggers and stop unhelpful thoughts and words before they came into my mind or out of my mouth. This helped to still my mind and allowed information and frequency to flow when it was ready to come through me.

But sometimes I would feel the overwhelm and enormity of my mission as a human being. I could feel the resistance of the ego and as you know, what you resist persists!

This led me to one of the biggest lessons I have learnt on my journey so far, we cannot tame the human ego by suppressing it, we must instead hold it in safe embrace, accept it, be kind to ourselves and allow the energy of compassion in to dissipate the loud and often insensitive voice of the ego.

The ego for many is essential in our reality, to navigate through the physical dimension as we do. For years it served as 'protection' because we thought we were not safe. The truth is that the perception of what it means to be safe has always been flawed. We are and always have been whole and safe, it is only our experiences that made us feel unsafe.

I realised early on that the frequency of Sentaura is here to call us back home to our hearts, to wholeness, and that is exactly what it did for me.

The kinder I was to myself, the quicker I was able to transmute lower frequencies and thought patterns. Each time I acknowledged the ego instead of suppressing it, I had another breakthrough which unravelled another piece of the Sentaura puzzle for me.

Indeed it was a puzzle, I would spend hours and hours in a meditative or trance state working with the frequency, downloading information, writing, drawing code, speaking light language, toning, and asking questions about Sentaura.

For more than two years, each night I would do self-healing and feel the warmth of Sentaura move through my own body. I was co-creating with it but wanted to understand more about it before sharing it with the world. I allowed the intelligence of the Sentaura frequency to teach me whilst I was also navigating the ups and downs of my human life.

The ego actually plays an important part in aiding our spiritual growth. Without the awareness of what our ego is feeling and experiencing through our emotions and physical bodies, we would not be able to ascend.

Acceptance of the ego is first of all necessary to prevent creating a negative and therefore problematic relationship with it.

So, it seems that we can choose to accept the ego and even befriend it to prevent resistance and make the process smoother.

Place your hands on your heart and tell yourself: "I am merging with the light" and send the ego some unconditional love and compassion.

In order to cultivate self-love, we must learn to love every single aspect of ourselves. After all, we are living a human experience and very few of us wake up enlightened.

For most of us, the merging of our Higher Self is a gradual process. For me, it happened very rapidly. I was aware of the importance of this work and was a woman with a mission and on a mission.

I fully trusted my Spirit guidance so spearheaded through energetic upgrades and life's challenges until I would often be so exhausted that all I could do was sleep. My physical body was being upgraded and alchemised and sleep would be the one thing that helped me integrate the energetic work my team was doing on me much more quickly.

As mentioned, there were times my body would burn with heat from these upgrades. It was not unbearable, it didn't hurt. Yes! It was a little uncomfortable but nothing a cool fan and a cold drink would not solve.

Over time the intensity of these energetic upgrades became less and less and made way for the most beautiful encounters with beings from all over the cosmos.

My frequency was being calibrated and with each vibrational calibration, I was able to access higher Source frequencies, dimensions, and different realms. Communication with these cosmic beings became easy and for some of them, I was the first "human" they ever connected with.

Coming Back to the "TRUE YOU"

The merging of our higher selves will happen at different times across the world, rapidly increasing as time passes. Sentaura along with the planetary alignments, and solar plasma waves are supporting our ascension and are attuning our bodies to higher frequencies which upgrade our genetic profile. These events and frequencies awaken the dormant energies and codes within every human being which hold information about our soul gifts and innate abilities.

It allows us to realise what is true for us and to assist humanity's awakening as a collective. As your energy amplifies and your abilities and soul gifts come 'online' you will need to know how to use them for the greater good, understand them and apply them so they can enrich your life and the lives of those around you. It is the 'gatekeeper' to you accessing even higher frequencies and streams of consciousness.

During our seven-month Sentaura training portal my students learnt much about their own abilities and soul gifts and how they could apply it in their work as healers. Kimberley realised that she could combine Kinesiology with Sentaura, co-create with the Fairy Kingdom and that it would completely change her life and healing work. Sharlene realised the potency and potential of her healing and innate ability to see code within plants and co-create with them and with Mother Gaia. Georgie realised that she was a channel for crystal wisdom and created powerful crystal grids and sacred transformational cacao ceremonies.

All these expressions of their soul are creating powerful healing ripples across the Earth. They could see the massive positive changes that were happening within them, within their relationships and their sacred healing work. During and after each initiation they would access more of their unique and innate way of healing and their soul wisdom. The Sentaura initiations were assisting them to amplify what was ready to come through them, in a BIG WAY!

Sentaura and your Higher Self facilitate the unification of your divine feminine and divine masculine energies, so it was a huge step for the Sentaura students to allow this unification. They simply had to trust and co-create with their Higher Self instead of fighting this return to wholeness. There was no turning back.

We as humans are on an upward trajectory and have been for a while. You have a choice to come along for the ride and embrace the adventures along the way so you can have a more intimate relationship with your higher soul self and your human self, have fulfilling sacred relationships with others, actively participate and engage fully in the spontaneous joy of co-creating life or you can choose to stay in a reality that keeps you locked in unhelpful patterns and fear for the sake of convenience.

Journal Prompt: Will you fully claim back your authentic self in this live and flowing experience called life? Write what you would like to claim back. Write it in the format I AM, as below. This is to acknowledge that you already ARE all you desire.

I am who I am because I AM!

I am the earth

I am the water

I am fire

I am wind

I am warrior

I am goddess

I am creatress

I am mother

I am friend

I am sister

I am soul

I am healer and alchemist

I am shaman and way shower

I am love

I am death

I am birth

I am fierce

I am gentle

I am strong

I am vulnerable

I am playful and passionate

I am universal intelligence

I am cosmic

I am Source

I am a Woman of the Divine!

I am a Woman of this Earth!

Within you I see me and within me I am you.

Beloveds connect with your I am

Rejoice in Her

Unearth the remembrance of your I AM

And all that she stands for.

For She is One, She is all of you, She is you.

Acknowledge When Your Soul Gifts Come 'Online'

In my work, I've seen many people's soul gifts come 'online' and they often feel very confused about their abilities. Know that it is completely normal in the times we live in. You are more magnificent than you could ever imagine.

The women who embarked on the Sentaura journey with me had a deep calling that they were here for more. They delved bravely into the broken connections they felt and in time built up confidence in their own gifts and abilities through their ever-deepening journey. They did not have all the answers but as time went on, they got to experience the expression of their soul in various ways which enriched their lives and the lives of those around them.

Sentaura helps us to become more attuned to ourselves, to the shifts in energy or mood, to sound, and to the pulse of the universe.

During and after Sentaura initiations and healing they could feel various sensations flowing through their physical body. Some were intense and some were pure bliss. Their body was a vehicle to explore their energy and emotions and embrace all the new parts of themselves that were coming 'online'. Their dormant codes were being activated and this made their souls come alive.

During Sentaura practice sessions, the divine intelligence of Sentaura would always bring new things to their attention to help shift their awareness around relationship with self, others or our planet.

The information shared during a Sentaura healing session is shared to enLIGHTen your life. Sentaura helps us to bravely step out of fear and explore, express, release and let ourselves be revealed—all the quirky bits, messy bits and the "I've got my sh*t together" bits that's been waiting for the moment to be acknowledged.

When you embrace the knowledge shared, I assure you, you will never look back and that is exactly what these students did.

They could see that by applying what they learned, fear could no longer live in their bodies and rule their energy.

Journal prompt: Are you here for more? What is that more? When you ask these questions where does fear arise in your body? Place your hands on that area and send it love. Ask your Higher Self to show you the block and the cause of this fear. Take a moment to journal your findings.

Flowing With Life, Not Against It

What Sentaura has taught me is that we are not meant to swim upstream. Flow arises when we release the emotional charge and fear codes held within us. When we flow our thinking, acting, feeling becomes an expression of the ever-flowing love of God, Source, our Creator.

Understand that you can access it anytime, anywhere and in any situation.

Love is YOU and you are Love.

Do not let anyone hold you back from your most beautiful life.

As a Keeper of the Light, you are here for these times.

You cannot mess things up.

You cannot get it wrong.

It is simply growth and deeper understanding of what makes you, YOU!

Keepers of the Light, claim this now:

I cannot and will not mess it up.

I will get through this.

It's ok to try new things and share my inspirations.

It's safe for me to share my sacred work with this world.

It's safe for me to follow my heart and divine intelligence.

I follow what feels supportive for me.

I embody my truth and take radical responsibility for my thoughts, my actions and my energy.

I am enough, more than enough.

I now tune out of fear and into love.

I now radiate fierce love to ignite the hearts of those who are ready to receive it.

My yes is my yes and my no is my no!

I trust the guidance of my higher self.

I express my infinite joy.

I am divine.

I am abundant.

I am strong and vulnerable at the same time.

I am LOVE!

And hold the light of creation within me.

All is well. Now and forever.

And so it is.

True Joy Comes from Loving Yourself Fiercely

True joy comes from sharing your love, your magic, medicine and wisdom with others.

It gives me great joy to hold space and guide people through their own profound transformations so they begin to radiate their own joy. Denying ourselves this joy denies a vital part of our aliveness, our connection to the web of life.

Light leaders, this is why you are here, to weave your love through the web of struggle and ignite the hearts of those that are ready to hear your voice and share in your energy.

Do you listen to your soul calling and wholeheartedly share what is ready to be expressed through you or do you say "Ugh! surely not me! I can't do that, who will listen?"

I had to let go of all that perceived BS so what was ready to come through me could and now I teach and initiate students in my sacred mystery school and guide them so they can share what they came here for.

Our human simply cannot comprehend the vastness of our infinite soul and we are plagued with unhelpful conditioning that's keeping us from truly sharing who we are.

Take some time to work through these questions below.

Journal Prompt: Do you easily give into the feeling of self-doubt which stops you from creating or do you claim back your fierce love for yourself?

What was the cause of this self-doubt?

Do your boundaries need a spruce up?

Do you give too much or lack direction and don't have time to let your creatress and creator fully anchor your sacred work in this world?

Are you believing that you do not deserve better?

Does the thought of you expanding into your next level greatness excite or scare you?

Are you stuck in a cycle of "not enough-ness"?

Are you suppressing the light, magic and medicine that is wanting to flow through you?

Perhaps you're ready to up-level your life and you're unsure where to start.

Perhaps you're ready to connect with the truest version of you and let your soul speak through you.

Perhaps you know you are so much more than what you believe yourself to be and want to know how to access that MORE!

Perhaps you are ready to love yourself fiercely and share that love so it ripples the change you want to see to those you work with?

You are the magic.

You are the change.

You are the wisdom.

You are the medicine.

Isn't it time you embrace and embody all that you are?

New Beginnings Are Afoot!

The beautiful transformations you're experiencing are creating space and an opening for a great unfoldment of your external world.

A world that you can gaze upon with pride in your heart.

The powerful beginnings and energy is a reminder that when you truly embody your I AM presence and act from a space of divine grace following your intuition, your Soul guidance, that you are able to create a life you love and manifest the blessings you desire.

Bring focus to your intentions and realign them with the guidance of your heart.

And remember who you really are.

Lean into life with gratitude and open eyes and say thank you to all you are and all that you have been.

Say thank you to all the parts of you that are already aligning and hold in sacred embrace those parts of you still integrating and healing.

Surrender a little deeper, accept a little more, honour your journey and each experience that is bringing you more into wholeness.

Feel into what you want to create next?

What is calling to you?

Feel your essence, your medicine flow through you.

Let yourself be heard. Allow yourself to speak of your love without apologizing for it.

Reclaim what is yours and step through the gateway that is open to us all.

Allow yourself to shift.

To be the embodiment of love and creation itself.

Let the truth within you shine bright.

You are your own magic.

The stage has been set for years now for this great spiritual awakening to unfold.

The curtains are open, and you are called to step forward on this stage called life.

Will you surrender and open your heart to all that is available to you?

Or will you shrink back in dismay and leave it for the "others" to take care of what is rightfully yours?

The more you live in the embodiment of the love within you, the more you can share that love in sacred service to others.

The opportunity is now.

All is unfolding exactly as it is meant to.

The choice is yours.

Will you follow the call within the deepness of your heart?

Trust the Process.

And remember the spark you've always carried within you that you can truly bring to the surface and live a conscious life steering and directing, igniting this spark in all aspects of your life.

And as you do ...

This shall truly inspire and empower you to lean deeper into what you came here to do.

And to share your beautiful, unapologetic, loving and truthful self.

You are so supported and loved, always.

NATALI BROWN

ABOUT THE AUTHOR

Natali is an international bestselling author, modern day alchemist, spiritual mentor and multi-dimensional channel, healer, Founder of The Divine Light Academy™, and Sentaura® Cosmic Ascension Energy Healing, and the creator of Spirit Talks™, a speaking platform for soul entrepreneurs.

Natali merges ancient wisdom, frequency and alchemy with modern times and initiate women and men to ignite the true expression of their creative soul through vibrational alchemy and channelled teachings. Her guidance reconnects them with their true inner authority and ignites their treasure trove of innate spiritual abilities, natural gifts and talents.

She helps leaders of change, healers, mystics, coaches, visionaries and soul entrepreneurs make the big moves to courageously step into their next level greatness, embody and express their soul essence, call in a new level of abundance and flow, and share their unique soul gifts with the world in a whole new way – guilt and shame free.

Living in New Zealand with her husband and two teenage boys she loves to explore and photograph the beauty of New Zealand.

Website:
https://natalibrown.com/

Facebook:
https://www.facebook.com/groups/AwakenedEmbodiedLightLeaders

Instagram:
https://www.instagram.com/natalibrown.sentaura/

A GLIMPSE INTO MY WONDERFUL COSMIC WORLD THAT IS SENTAURA

GEORGINA CURNOW

2

Where to start? It is hard to decide what to single out from the many expansive, powerful, transformational, and often indescribable experiences I had throughout the seven-month container, which was the first Sentaura Practitioner training facilitated by Natali.

I have decided to take you right back to the very beginning because it shows the important transitions and process of transformation I've gone through. It also sets the scene and shows you just how far I have come with the help, support and healing of Sentaura, Natali and my Sentaura SiStars.

Before Natali crossed my path and Sentaura entered my consciousness I was unsure of a lot of things, my purpose, my place in this life and my gifts. I knew what my passions were but could not yet see how it all fitted into the puzzle of all that is, the flow of life and oneness, the reason for being here.

I understood the concept of 'oneness' but had yet to truly feel it or feel part of it. I still did not 'believe' despite all that I knew, have learnt and experienced. I was frustrated at my perceived lack of connection and ability to hear and feel my guides and Source.

I felt like I knew a lot, compared to four years previously, and was beginning to tap into the universal wisdom of Source but was not embodying it. I did not feel solid in myself, in who I was or what I was capable of, but I could feel the potential sitting there, waiting patiently for me to claim it.

I have always had an amazing ability to lean into fear, embrace change and take on new experiences. Especially, if I have a sense that they are going to enable me to evolve further.

This has always served me well, as long I am also listening to my heart and picking what is right and in alignment with me. Saying

'Yes' to Sentaura was an easy no-brainer in the respect that I had an immediate full body, all in YES!

I remember this pivotal moment vividly—the sunshine was beaming through the windows during this early afternoon. We had just sat in sacred circle, some of my best friends and soul star sisters were around me. I was feeling centred, peaceful and present. Natali began to talk for the very first time about this frequency called Sentaura that she was bringing into this world. At the time she shared what she knew, as she was downloading information from her Spirit Team piece by piece.

About three sentences in, I could feel the tears welling up and then they began to stream, warm trickles down my cheeks. Very happy, heart singing and grateful tears. It was an immediate soul recognition, remembrance and activation and it felt like my heart was overwhelmingly huge. Full of so much relief, gratitude, celebration and love all at once. I wasn't sure I could hold it all. Was I going to explode or worse implode?! I don't even remember much of what was said, just a massive sense of "I've been waiting for this for a very long time". So, when Natali revealed that she would be offering Sentaura Practitioner training for Healers, initiating them to the Sentaura Creator Frequency, it was a definite full body and soul 'YES!' for me.

I could feel the immensity of this frequency—the change and transformation it would bring to humanity and to our world, its sacredness, magic, the pure unconditional love of this divine frequency, its wisdom and strength, and the reverence and responsibility that was going to accompany it all—it scared the pants off me!

Even though it was an initial full body yes, I didn't rush the decision to join the training program. My ego was doing its job and trying its very best to keep me safe and comfortable right where I was. Those pesky limiting questions started to arise: "How can I be worthy of this sacred, special, Earth and humanity changing frequency, energy and work? Am I experienced enough? Am I capable of holding this incredible gift and doing it justice and understanding the responsibility required?" I knew this was a pivotal turning point and an important crossroads for me. There was no right or wrong answer, but it was one of those life choices that are few and far between, maybe even lifetimes apart!

Generally, if something scares the pants off me and it's not life-threatening, then it is always a clear sign that I am walking in the right direction and that my edges are flying swiftly towards me; waiting for me to take that uncertain leap of faith, off the cliff edge into the unknown. Again, I found myself standing on this familiar edge—the tips of my toes already hanging over. The fear I felt was visceral, very physical, sudden pains, sick to the stomach nausea and tremors. A deep fear that I was nowhere near worthy enough. Anxiety began creeping in, "What if I don't see as much as everyone else?" or "What if I can't feel the energy at all?"

I felt like the newbie on the block as my 'awakened' journey only began four years previously. Literally coming from a sceptical, scientifically atheist mindset to this point. It doesn't get more 'out there' than a completely new cosmic modality! And here I was considering working with this ancient frequency, a completely unknown new energy healing system, creative, life transforming frequency! But I have nurtured a sound ability to see and recognise these idiosyncrasies of the ego and culture of self-doubt. I thanked my unhelpful stories and then politely asked them to dissipate and used it as an opportunity to shed yet another layer.

Of course, the polar opposite arose during the training in organic moments of pure gratitude, joy, hope and sheer full-hearted happiness. I felt a massive sense of self-pride, this was no small undertaking. My warrior rose tall. My goddess gleamed, shimmering in gold. My wise old soul began to slowly unfurl and the child in me, who always wanted to be first a magician and then an astrologer, laughed and reminded me that this was a missing aspect of me returning and that I had been waiting for it. The universe was handing me my permission and confirmation ticket for all I had forgotten to be true.

My five-year-old self knew there was so much more to life, but school and society had successfully knocked out any belief in the unseen. Instead, it had installed a need for proof or reasoning of anything magical or that held mystery. I had forgotten and didn't even realise these parts of me were missing.

When I reflect on it, I can now see for all those years, I felt there was something more to the universe. Something that was beyond my human comprehension. But I didn't know what it was. I felt curious and very drawn to it but did not want to be 'taken for a fool to believe in the weird woo woo'. I was just floating patiently in the background of a busy life—sceptical, analytical and atheist. However, I have always had this strong sense that there was so much we don't know or actually it is that we don't remember! There is way more to life, the universe, and our capability, than what we have been allowed to know.

And so here I was about to step off the force-fed pages of my life for good and I was so exceedingly excited! My tiny spark that had been sitting in the dark waiting, had been reignited, refuelled and was raring to get to work.

And so, I took a giant leap and said yes and it wasn't long before the first Sentaura initiation began to drift towards us.

During the week leading up to the first initiation, I shed countless tears and felt very exposed and vulnerable. I was feeling all the polarity feels from moment to moment. They ranged from extra cuddly with my family, needing space, sad, on a high, angry, frustrated, peaceful, calm, trapped, free but incredibly compassionate towards everything, myself included. It was like a higher understanding had begun to settle in. The Sentaura vibration had started to adjust my frequencies already.

My senses felt amplified and my perspective on what was going on in the outside world sharpened. I found myself gauging situations around me, watching them play out and I had a deep knowing that they would all work out ok. Everything was as it should be.

Many ideas started to drop in, I was excited and yet, I had this feeling of tranquillity, knowing that the right time would present itself for me to put my ideas into action. I have learnt quite a few lessons about divine timing and how everything happens at the perfect time. I began to feel a stillness and calmness settling in. Was this a moment of serenity before the storm?

It was the evening before starting our seven-month initiation and training journey with Natali. The chilly winter sunset was stunning with a strip of bright, zesty orange, merging into a sunny, joyful yellow, before merging into a bottle green that dissolved into the deep blue night sky. It was magnificent to behold as if Mama Earth and Father Sky were letting me know that something very special was occurring. The star Sirius was high and bright, twinkling at me knowingly. I sat by our cosy, smouldering fire feeling the warm comforting incandescence on my face from the flames.

I held my cup of sacred beloved Mama Cacao to my heart. As always, I set my intention, offering gratitude and appreciation, calling in and honouring the elements, the earth, the sky, the sun, the moon, all ancestors and higher vibrational beings of light to protect, guide, support and love me. After mindfully sipping my ceremonial cacao, I burnt my prewritten list of all the aspects I was ready to let go of and release. It went up in smoke quickly, little sparks flying upwards, zig-zagging in a flash then gone.

I pulled cards from my new deck which arrived that day. Divine timing. I chuckled at the humour and wisdom I always receive from my guides. The messages reminded me of my commitment to trust and to have faith, and my devotion to sacred union.

I gifted myself a heavenly salt bath infused with aromatic rose petals and soft flickering candlelight. My sacrum had been 'burning hot' on and off all evening which was a first. And I felt a beautiful angel energy present, something I've not experienced before either. Going to bed that evening, I felt very calm, peaceful, slightly fizzy (my cells were upgrading already) and so very supported and held.

I journaled that evening, "I always knew I was here for something special, and this feels exactly like it is a major part. Sentaura, an ambassador of light, pure unconditional love and light. Which is what I am. It is such an honour to be here in my sovereignty, to assist with creating the New Earth and receiving the highest of frequencies. I feel very humbled and grateful". And so, my journey began.

I remember very little from our first initiation. I dropped in and out, 'asleep' but not, if that makes sense. What I do remember are small pieces of the experience. A feeling of unfathomable infinite love. I was gifted armour of stunning silver fabric weaved from light which moved like liquid. A water code 'dropped in' and flowed around me, and I saw millions of lights that were souls I believe to be here on Earth.

When I reflected on it later in the day, I felt disappointed that I didn't see more. Even though I knew that my experience was perfect as it was. Natali had told me that during the initiation I went quite high dimensionally and I have since learned that sometimes when this happens my human self tends to just 'check out' and rest whilst my soul takes the front seat.

I could sense a lot of adjustment and movement within my body that evening. My human thought it was all a bit too good to be true! That somehow the Universe had made a mistake and I had been picked to do this work by accident. Of course, I know this was not true but my soul had been waiting for this for so long, it felt too good to be real! What an eye, heart and soul-opening adventure this was going to be.

Embodying My Divine Sovereignty

Below are the words that flowed from me, only two weeks into the Sentaura Practitioner Program, when we were asked to write our declaration of sovereignty. This was a hugely significant key moment of freedom of expression for me. A moment where I could actually express my heart's whispers and Sentaura helped me to do just that.

This was the moment when I truly began to accept and embody the powerful, creative sovereign individual that I really am and always have been. It is a moment of sheer celebration in my achievement of following my heart, allowing, trusting and surrendering, over and over again, and continuing to do so still, meeting edge after edge after edge.

I am here.

I am Eliyjha (Eee-lee-ya)

A Goddess of Light

I claim and own my full light and love potential now.

I dissolve all fear, doubt, mistrust and ego based survival constructs, through all time, space, multi-dimensions and realities now.

I fully embody and feel fully my light, my love, my gifts, my integrity, my compassion, my joy, my pleasure and playfulness. Surrendering all control and fully stepping into trust of the divine, oneness, unity and connection.

I claim my ancient wisdom, lessons and knowledge back now and the remembrance of who I am and who Be in my true core.

I am love, I am light

I am strength and courage

I am an anchor and have the capacity to hold limitless love and light for myself, loved ones, our Mother Earth and Humanity.

I am here to stand for freedom, liberation, healing, unconditional love, light, justice, truth, empowerment, integrity, joy and authenticity.

I am here to stand for the liberation of linear understanding, limiting beliefs, patriarchy and constricted sacred divine feminine and divine masculine energies.

I am here to hold, heal and support our Mother Earth and all divine energetic beings.

I stand for the freedom of abundance, fruition and rich thriving of all plants, creatures, sentient beings and Mother Earth.

I anchor my light now deep within our Earth and high into the cosmos, connected to all, alongside my sisters and brothers that are of the highest integrity and truth and that are here to help create the New Earth.

I serve only from my heart and in pure love and light.

I declare and claim my power and sovereignty back with every cell of my being.

And so it is.

Reading what I wrote then, literally blows me away and it feels like my heart cracks wide open each time I read it! To give you some perspective, this is not how I have ever written before this point.

From the age of four I have struggled to express myself verbally and spent about eighty-five percent of my life with a thoroughly blocked throat chakra. It was physically painful for me to express my feelings. Many times, not even being able to get words out at all. They just stuck and felt like a tight ball in my throat.

From the age of nine, I labelled myself as being dyslexic, having been tested at seven and the results were inconclusive. I wasn't diagnosed then until I was seventeen. I had spent the four years before Sentaura, consciously peeling away the multiple layers and walls around my voice and my heart. Relearning how to feel that it was safe to express my emotions and truth, and learning to accept and love my voice. I always disliked my voice and felt embarrassed at its low tone, but now I truly love my voice and own my frequency.

I have come a long way but of course, there is always work to do. For me to write something like this and now also this chapter, which is worded eloquently with grace and full of so much passion, love and heartfelt truth, is really very phenomenal for me indeed.

It is almost unbelievable. Words just flow out onto the page, and I feel lit up, ignited, and full of joy and excitement whilst writing them! This is an absolute confirmation of just how powerful the alchemical, creative energy of Sentaura is and just how quickly it works. Instantaneously! It has opened up a door of gushing creativity and self-expression to the point where I have a 'word frequency' antenna within me now. This enables me to feel the vibration of a single word or sentence. My creative self-expression continues to flow and expand, not only with the written word but also through events, sounds, music and movement. I know there is a lot more to come and the frequency of Sentaura is incredibly supportive in opening up the freedom for this to flow in. It has become an integral part of my daily life.

Out Of This World Initiation Experiences

During the seven-month container we were initiated to twenty-four different Sentaura Royal Creator Codes™. Every single one was completely different, and I had a whole variety of unique in-body and out-of-body experiences, that ranged from drifting into a world of higher consciousness, to incredibly vivid inter-dimensional experiences, seeing different realms, indescribable visions, meeting many new light energetic beings, receiving various cosmic gifts and energetic armour. And one of the most humbling experiences was being in the direct presence of divine Source and feeling gratitude from all the light beings for the work we do. This happened right at the conclusion of training and sometimes after our Earth healing sessions.

There are no words that can describe the heart-filling, soul-shining appreciation that we have received. So it is tricky to choose just a couple of initiations because they were all out of this world amazing, but I have chosen two that hold a special place in my heart.

The Sentaura Creator Key Code of Joy™ is definitely one of my favourites. I even have a silk print of it on my fridge. When I first saw it my eyes lit up and my heart swelled. I did not want to stop looking at it. As with all the codes, it drew me in and I could feel a massive soul smile expanding and shining inside of me.

For me, this initiation was a very physical in-body experience. As I gazed at it, what I felt in my heart space was beauty, grace, peace and heart love. I felt Sentaura begin to flow into my sacral chakra, almost like butterflies fluttering. This sensation weaved its way up to my solar plexus and then to my heart, swirling and settling there. I felt patches of gentle throbbing pain come and go in my lower back, in my left ovaries and right ankle.

Shivers trickled across my right shoulder as a block dissolved from my throat. I could see the code enter every single cell in my body which was mind-boggling and hard for my human mind to grasp. It felt so joyful, and my heart expanded outwards.

After the initiation, it took a little while for me to 'come back to Earth'. This is not an unfamiliar feeling with this high frequency deep healing Sentaura work. I often heard my friends say afterwards: "You're not quite back, are you?!" And I was often incredibly hungry afterwards and could have eaten a horse! (Excuse the olde English metaphor!). It was my body's way of saying, "Please ground me back down and get your feet back on the Earth!" I was buzzing with delight and super excited to feel so alive, and full of so much love and joy!

As I mentioned before, I was not fully conscious during all the initiations. There were a few where I fell 'asleep', and my human mind was blissfully resting. I found these times quite frustrating as I do love to journey and experience the magical unknown worlds.

However, the Sentaura Pleasure Code™, womb wisdom and yoni consciousness initiation were completely the opposite and an incredibly transformational journey.

For this initiation, Natali asked us to choose a crystal that represented our goddess energy and said that it was going to accompany us. Now crystals are definitely right up there as one of my many life's loves. I am a crystal wisdom keeper and healer and have been collecting them since I was seven. So, I had a fair few to choose from as you can imagine! It was actually a very quick and easy decision. I chose my stunning natural Citrine point that came from the Congo. It was radiating abundance, joy and golden light, and was an obvious choice by my Goddess.

When guided, I stepped straight into my goddess energy. This was a first, I have always wrestled a bit with this aspect of myself. However today it was delightfully easy! I saw my golden goddess light rise up. My fierce warrior aspect was sat high on her horse. She had golden armour as light as silk and her sword of light sheathed on her back. I could also sense my gentle maiden, with her quiet, grounded strength of presence and peace.

When I gazed at the code, I felt excited like a child in a sweet shop, with wide innocent eyes, exhilaration, and eagerness. Physically I felt it fizzing in my sacral chakra and this created an inspired, motivated, happy and joyous sensation. We connected with our womb consciousness.

Mine had been waiting for acknowledgment. Bless! It is our creative and abundance centre and the message I received is that we will now finally work together instead of being separate. Unified, complete and whole in our creativity.

Natali guided us into the visual meditation, and I found myself arrive at a very powerful, flowing blue river. Myself, Natali, Kimberley and Sharlene were guided to a more gentle part of this river, where we waded in up to our waists. We stood holding hands in sacred circle, the water swirling gently around and in between us. I felt vulnerable but not uncomfortable. I saw us holding more light than in human form.

Each of us took turns to be gently held by the women in the group, allowing the water to wash over us, cleanse and flow right through us. It took with it any old trauma, dense energy, beliefs of shame, guilt, secretiveness, and self-disgust. Anything that was no longer serving our divine goddess sovereignty.

Each women's water healing that day was very different, stunningly unique and visual poetry in motion. I allowed myself to be held, something that does not come easily for me. The Sirian beings came in and surrounded us, bringing with them codes of light. Natali said she could hear a symphony of sound and see electric blue waves surrounding me, but stillness everywhere else.

I had the sensation of waves, and I could see the blue light but could not hear the sounds. I saw floating music notes instead. When I stood up, I was electric blue, like an Avatar! And I had a sparkling, blue crystal and diamond crown on my head. I felt strong, powerful in presence, the joy of pleasure and the freedom to feel it without guilt or shame.

Holding space for and celebrating my beautiful SiStars, I saw Sharlene rise as a golden, sparkling, powerful goddess being. Kimberley stood radiating a beautiful pink light, surrounded by floating flowers and petals and Natali I saw as radiating, a powerful, shimmering platinum silver light, expanding in all directions.

It was such an incredibly empowering, healing and nurturing moment for each of our souls. I felt it truly cemented our connection, trust and unconditional love for each other. Something that I had not thought of prior to this journey, was the soul family I would gain. I am immensely grateful for this.

The experiences and what we have been through and have shared together have created a bond that is unbreakable, by vicinity, time and dimensions. I hold so much love and gratitude for my Sentaura SiStars that words will never be enough to describe it. But they know! Cue heartfelt tears, ha-ha I can definitely be called the teary one of the group!

Organic Multi-faceted Event

I cannot possibly fit into this single chapter all the variations of healing, transformations and experiences that happened to me. So, I have very carefully chosen a select few of my most powerful and profound ones. We all know and love how the universe works in mysterious ways and I experienced this first hand many times during my Sentaura journey.

I am not sure if there is a name for an impromptu healing, transmutation, process, clearing, understanding and upgrading that happens completely out of the blue, anywhere or at any time, so I am going to call it an 'organic multi-faceted event'.

I had quite a few of these, most of them actually happened whilst driving! Do not worry it did not impede my ability to drive safely. Lol. When my mind and body are automatically occupied with driving, this allows space for my subconscious to come forward, to be seen and heard unhindered.

One such event happened only one month into the Sentaura program. I had an amazing one-on-one healing session with Natali. We had cleared some old beliefs, programs, stories of lack and self-trust, and finished with embodying my essence of joy, so I was feeling really good and bright-eyed.

Driving to school pick up afterwards I received a text message from a friend. I had missed my daughter receiving a certificate in her school assembly. This triggered a huge healing process. I suddenly became so incredibly angry at not being told about this by the school as I could have been there if I had known. To put it into perspective, it is a once-in-a-year occurrence, and I was gutted that I missed this special moment.

My family comes first one hundred percent and rage bubbled up as I was getting closer to school. I could feel that there was a lot more happening within me than just being cross from missing out. So, I pulled into the car park and tried to release some of the stewing rage through muscle tensing and sound. I began to use conscious breathing to get back to my centre. Through breathing, I asked myself questions: "Why was this having such a massive impact on my nervous system?" I am a compassionate person and I used to be a teacher, I know how busy things get! "What was the lesson or learning here for me?"

I called my husband and spilled out all my emotions, I felt so upset and tears began to stream. I was physically trembling, and my heart was really hurting. The situation was completely out of my control. I did not know about this presentation. Why did this feel so painful and what was causing this to bubble up?

And then it hit me really hard, I had to surrender and accept—that old chestnut! The simple and realistic fact that I cannot always be there for my children, dawned on me, like a heavy axe landing. There was a huge aspect of me having to let go. Then the core aspect of all this trauma dropped in, it was Mother-Daughter wounding. When I was young there was a lack of attention and affection from my own Mother. I do not hold this against Mum in any way, I'm one of five and she often had two jobs. I have no idea how she did it all! I knew I needed to dig a little deeper and called in Mother Isis for support and help. I then voice messaged Natali.

As I talked, what came through was that I was transmuting a collective ancestral wound. I could feel the hearts of all mothers that wanted to be there for their children, but they were not able to be, for one reason or another. All of their accumulated guilt, shame and belief of failure. This required acknowledgment, understanding, acceptance and forgiveness—it was ready to dissolve.

I called in my team and the Seraphim to bring in the Sentaura energy and support to help transmute and clear this. Using breathwork and light language I allowed healing, forgiveness, unconditional love and compassion to flow in and sent it out into all lineages, then around and through the Earth. The pain started to ebb, and my system began to relax and calm. I had a lot of gentle tears streaming, but no sobbing or drama. They were tears of compassion, gratitude, relief and sheer humility that I could do this not only for myself and my children but en masse for the collective and the ripple effect that it would have. It was overwhelming and I still find it hard to believe.

The thing that still always blows me away with Sentaura is that the healing is just so powerful and really quick! No drama or fluffiness attached. This process all happened in the space of about twenty minutes. I did feel very vulnerable and energetically open afterwards, and the integration of all this healing is a different story because my glorious human body and mind takes a wee while to catch up. I was what I call, "dog tired" later that afternoon and physically could not do anything else but sleep.

We are taught to believe things must be complicated and long-winded. When really once we begin to master our own awareness and energy, there is no reason why we cannot heal instantly. It is only our belief system that stops us from doing it. After writing about this experience in my journal I stated,

"I AM FUCKING AWESOME AND A FORCE TO BE RECKONED WITH!"

And beautiful reader, so are you! It is only layers, stories and beliefs that lie between you and your true potential power and that is the delightful journey of being human.

As you can see my journey to self-mastery is not always a box of fluffy, rainbows and unicorns. In particular this journey with Sentaura, it felt like I was in a constant death and rebirth cycle, after cycle! But that is what happens when you are constantly upgrading and choosing to evolve.

About two months into the program, I was ready to call a time-out and this is what I journaled at the time: "Fuck off world. Fuck off spirituality. Fuck off knowing better. Fuck off understanding!" I wanted to be on holiday and blissfully unaware of any truth. It had been a rough week and I was questioning everything, 'the usuals' as I now call them: "What am I doing? Why am I even here? Is this even real?!" A very familiar place to be. I'm sure you will resonate with this place if you have done any inner work on yourself before. I felt flat, low and unmotivated. I just wanted to sleep, do nothing and not be disturbed!

My journal reads: "All I want to do is have a break. We have initiation tomorrow and normally I feel excited but right now I just want to rest—long term. I feel cross and overwhelmed. It is all too much to keep up with. My human self feels like a rag doll being pushed and pulled in so many different directions. I feel like I can't keep up". Old parts of me were putting up a good fight.

I voiced this to my soul SiStars in the group and within ten minutes it began to dissolve. Natali reminded us to always voice and share our feelings as this is the first step of letting go and releasing. I immediately came back to my centre and my sense of humour returned. This was a beautiful example of just how fast simply acknowledging your state and thought pattern can transmute the energy instantly. We are not our emotions; it is just energy moving in motion.

Not being attached and holding onto things can dissipate them instantly. Something I have learned about myself during this time is that when I feel like this, it almost always means something significant is going to occur. When I feel flat and question, "What the fuck am I doing and why?" that is my sign that another death and rebirth cycle was occurring. I became very good at recognising these moments, especially towards the end of the program.

As the law of polarity is infinitely present, there were many high moments as well.

Here is a quote from my journal that I wrote after an initiation. It is how I often felt afterwards:

"I feel so free, lighter and liberated, with so much more joy, love, compassion and understanding for myself. I am a lot calmer, centred and solid and feel immense gratitude, peace, and completely renewed—like a new-born baby. I feel much lighter and somehow different. I am able to hear my Spirit Guides more clearly and trust myself more, I feel invincible!!"

Healing our Blessed Mother Earth

Once a month all Sentaura Practitioners gather to combine our skills and light to help heal our Mother Earth in any way that we can. This is completely guided in the moment and takes many different forms. We astral travel to do this work. It is one of my most favourite aspects of being a Sentaura practitioner. We don't only do this once a month, as individuals we also do it whenever we feel called to as well. It is always very healing for us too.

Here is one such experience:

The definition of discipline is: *"The practice of training to obey rules or a code of behaviour, using punishment to correct disobedience"*. This goes against every single cell in my being but I have long held the belief that I would benefit from having more discipline. It is what society and often leaders suggest that is good for us!

For me my belief of being disciplined was getting to bed early, being able to get up early to meditate, do some yoga, write my journal, and plan my day—all before the kids get up and the school rush begins.

In reality, I am well known for going to bed extremely late, and have done so since I was a teen, then pressing the snooze button a couple of times before getting up in a mad panic to get to school on time. Although I love to exercise and know how amazing it makes me feel, I do not always use this tool regularly enough.

I also fully understand my addiction to sugar and comfort eating and how it makes me feel. I have lifted myself from it many times and yet I find myself still leaning on this distraction. You can see why I might feel that a bit of discipline might benefit me and why I was giving myself a hard time about it.

However, when I read the definition of discipline it went against every single thing I believe to be true.

This incongruency raised its ugly head during a Sentaura Earth Healing session, four months in. Just one of many examples of a shadow aspect sitting dormant in my subconscious, that was ready to be dissolved and released—an old belief that was cultural and generational.

I grew up believing that to have discipline was a good thing, something to be proud of. I saw myself as never really having any at all and felt a constant sense of failure because of it. Not meeting my own high unrealistic expectations and 'should be's'. As long as I had this belief, I would never be good enough in my eyes.

For this particular Earth Healing we were in a sacred circle, in my healing room, the calming aroma of white sage and Palo Santo hanging in the air. A crystal grid lay in the centre, created with Selenite, Seraphinite, Sodalite and shimmering Aura Quartz.

As Natali lead the guided Earth healing, I gave myself the permission to let it be transmuted, dissolved and to let go of this outdated belief. During the visualisation, I saw myself sitting crossed-legged, surrounded by nature.

Bright beautiful green lush grass, shimmering in the sun, birds singing everywhere, the trees' leaves rustling in the gentle warm breeze and a fresh earthy smell arose from the ground when you took in a deep breath. It felt peaceful, sitting here on the Earth. I was humming and holding space with an open heart. My Sirian guides came in bringing blue light codes and white light began to stream from my heart outwards. We were working with the mountains and matrix. I saw many cracks opening within the mountains and the light began flooding through. As a group, we began to dissolve the veil. We were freeing and unbinding the mountains, as well as my heart.

It is difficult to describe fully what happens during the healings or initiations because a lot of it, our gorgeous human minds cannot comprehend, but our higher soul knows. I can often feel my higher self merge with my body but cannot quite express this feeling in words. This is yet another lesson in surrendering deeper into trust and faith, in the divine, knowing that all is as it is meant to be and for the highest greatest good, even if we often do not always understand it.

I suddenly started coughing a lot. I felt little waves of irritation and a lot of blue Sirian energy swirling in my solar plexus. Sentaura was clearing more layers from my expression centre which is the throat chakra. Light language started flowing freely from me. My heart and soul singing together of healing, old wisdoms and unconditional love. I do not always know the meaning of the frequencies that flow through me, but this time it felt like a soothing blanket of love, like a balm, with the intention of gently reaching all the hearts of all leaders and then to all of humanity.

We were then softly guided back by Natali and I remember a slight resistance to wanting to come back. The frequencies that we are in the presence of during our Sentaura circles can be very high and blissfully peaceful. It feels like home, and I always feel very supported, loved and held.

It turned out that it was devotion that I was looking for not discipline. The devotion to loving myself just as much as I love, care and share with others. It is almost like I have been activated in writing this piece, it has triggered a renewal of self-devotion to flow in. I am prioritising the self-care of my body and space. A new cycle has begun. Things are very simple when you trim away the excess of your mind and all the outside influences.

I offer healing to Mother Earth almost daily. It is an honour to be able to contribute to the well-being of our planet and all who reside here. It is often in the form of light language and sacred coding. Always bringing in and anchoring more light, dissolving, recoding or transmuting. We all have the potential to make positive ripples. Just sing to nature, share your joy and love. It is that simple.

Divine Gifts Received with a Gracious Heart

We are made of the Earth, stardust and threads of light. We are all made of the same building blocks as the entire universe. It is all within us, but it helps our human self to get to grips with the task of BEing, if we sometimes have a little help.

During all the initiations, Earth healing missions, activations and one-on-one mentoring with Natali we received so many blessings, healing and soul gifts.

Here are just a few of the gifts I had the honour of receiving during my time working with Natali and the divine frequency of Sentaura.

A Rose Quartz was placed into my heart for expanded unconditional love, compassion and forgiveness. Beautiful, stunning feathers were added to my wings. A sword of freedom. The alchemy of sacred geometry. A diamond from the Fairy Queen. A scroll with words and codes was placed into my throat from Melchizedek.

A tiny seed placed on my palm revealed a crack with light shining out, which then disappeared into the centre of my palm. This allows me to plant people right where they are, to ground their roots, nurture their remembrance, trust and faith within themselves. To nurture and empower growth and to support the planting of seeds of truth.

Being 'reborn' was an experience I view as a gift in itself. During another visualisation journey, which is difficult to describe due to its enormity, I was shown a doorway and golden mist that was the representation of divine Source. I looked closer and was shown a cosmic explosion, much like the big bang and was taken back to the beginning of creation.

I was then shown in a split second the whole history of time. I felt myself rise up through higher dimensions and I did not want to come back down to Earth. My conscious self knows this was epic beyond words and I trust that my soul understands it!

I also experienced an upgrade which I am going to call an 'I am' awakening. It helped me understand and feel just how I am connected to everything, and everything is connected to me. Every time I looked or saw something I heard: "I am".

For instance, I saw a hawk soaring in the sky and felt a deep sense that 'I am him and he is me'. I felt a deep connection with plants as I put soil around them. How can I expect it to grow if I don't feed it? This was making me reflect on my own sense of self-care. I noticed Bumble bees on rosemary flowers in the sunshine, busy busy. A dead fly on the windowsill, not so glamorous, but it is life. I noticed Mowzer, my cat who gently whiled her day away sleeping. The epitome of knowing just what she needs in any given moment.

I am all of this and it is all part of me. It is almost overwhelming and mind-boggling to think how connected we are and at the same time and it gave me great comfort and understanding.

During one incredibly important personal healing session with Natali, which had a few parts to it, I received back my innocence, beauty and magic. What a massive relief that was! It was an immensely painful process. I had to travel back along my timeline to the thirteenth century. I was being attacked in a dark forest and my soul light and innocence were stolen from me.

I felt a huge ball of anger, sadness, lack of safety and tremendous injustice. But it was time for forgiveness and healing. I claimed back my love, my heart, my spark and my long, so long-lost innocence. I gifted healing, forgiveness and self-love back to those who had wronged me. Again, not a process that was easy, but I was so held and supported all the way through it.

It was also revealed that I had made vows in past lifetimes, never to use my magic for the dark arts again. This needed dissolving because it was blocking me from accessing my magic in this lifetime.

I declared that: "I will never use my magic ever again for the dark. I now and always will only use my magic for the greatest and highest good of love and light always". With these powerful words and Natali's amazing alchemist healing abilities, another block was cleared! Amazing!

I then travelled back to my five-year-old self in this lifetime. I had given away my voice and the freedom to be me. Acknowledging this, I accepted into my heart a bright, sparkly flower. This was my joy, and a golden, twinkling, luminescent ball of light, that was my magic. I was dancing inside, and I finally felt whole again.

It is funny how you know that something is missing but you cannot tell what it is until it returns.

These are the words that came through after the healing session:

For so long

She has remained contained

She has been restrained

Trapped in a never-ending cycle, lost innocence.

That integral piece of missing heart.

Lost in the woods.

Looking searching

Trying to fill the gap, a hole.

Impossible to fill.

Unjustly ripped away

One fateful day

In a moment.

And now you have been found

I claim you back with wide open arms.

A grateful heart

Peace. Stillness. Love.

Is all she ever wanted.

My First Time Hands-On Sentaura Healing

During our training we first practiced doing our Sentaura healing on each other.

Kimberley was my first and I was frightfully nervous and apprehensive. The 'what ifs' came back into play at the back of my mind, and I just wanted to run in the opposite direction.

Sharlene and I had done our pre-hands-on protocol and Kimberley was comfortably lying on her back on the massage bed. I was drawn to her feet first, so gently held my fingertips there and tuned in. I was hoping like crazy I would feel something and then swiftly reminded myself to trust and clear my mind.

I let Sentaura work its magic. I felt a massive relief, breathed, and just surrendered. I began to feel the energy move through me. I felt and experienced so much all of a sudden. Before Sentaura I did Ascension Reiki healing as a Reiki Master, but this felt very different, much more potent.

I picked up on pain that was across her chest and stomach. I addressed this and then became aware of a tribal guide standing beside her. Sharlene also confirmed this. He was wearing a lot of feathers, which made me think North American Indian perhaps.

He was happily dancing, and his message was one of joy and for her to bring more of it into her life. Next, I was aware of pain in her head which I started to shift but due to the enormity of this block, I needed a little of Natali's help and guidance to do so and within seconds, it shifted. Success!

My first Sentaura practice healing was amazing once I let go of my own fear. I felt a sense of relief after the session was done. I felt so good, clearer, brighter, very supported and loved. With each healing since I have grown in confidence and always feel way better after the healing session.

Because we channel the Sentaura energy with the help of the Seraphim and Diamond Light, we also receive healing at the same time. How wonderful and blessed is that? There are just so many reasons to love being a Sentaura Practitioner.

In practicing, I have learnt that I feel first in my own body what is happening for my client. I use light language, recoding, hand movements, breath and intuitive visualization during my sessions. Every client I have healed with Sentaura always says they feel incredibly relaxed. Some see colours, visions or meet their guides, sometimes for the first time. All receive messages for their benefit, and all speak of having a really good sleep the night of their healing.

One client had injured herself badly and had not had a full night's sleep for six weeks since it had happened. After her healing, she slept the whole night through for the first time. For other clients I have unshackled them from chains of old vows that have been holding them back. Transmuted shadows. Lifted layers and blocks away from the heart to make space to be able to receive love and forgiveness. I have noticed that nearly every client has benefited from a lot of clearing and reconnecting to their solar plexus, which is their power centre.

This is not surprising in the times we live in. I have reconnected clients' light columns back into the Earth and unblocked their third eye chakras. Often Mother Gaia sings through me with light language of reassurance, safety, love and support and shares the message that we are safe to be in our bodies. I use rainbow light bridges to connect chakras that are misaligned or not 'communicating' with each other. During healings I also sometimes use my crystals. They assist me with clearing, reactivating and raising the frequency.

I love to hear from my clients how Sentaura helps them in so many different ways. The feedback I have received is that they feel much lighter, like a load has been lifted off them. They feel brighter within themselves, and they feel 'more' themselves again. They speak of having more clarity, motivation, energy, and a renewed sense of hope.

Every single healing is completely different and as unique as the individual lying on the table. An open heart, clear mind and full trust are so important for me to be able to hold the amazing healing space I do.

How Has Sentaura Influenced My Life and BEing?

I find myself struggling to express the answer to this question because the answer is so expansive. I am fully aware that at my core and soul level, I am who I am, and nothing can ever change that. However, there is not a single aspect of my life that hasn't been touched by the positive energy of Sentaura. It has facilitated my healing, unblocking, activating, remembrance, protection, support and love for my human self unconditionally.

So many layers have been shed, that who I BE is a lot closer to the surface now. It has amplified, realigned and strengthened my connection with my higher self, the stars, the elements, my crystals, mother nature and so much more. My eyes see brighter (literally one eye has improved according to the optician). I feel more at peace than I have ever done, which let's be honest, in these times is not short of a miracle.

My relationship with my husband and children has improved dramatically. I express myself more fully and communicate boundaries with ease. I have greater compassion, enjoy having fun and bring more playfulness into my day. I dance and sing more often. I basically remember to enjoy life a whole lot more!

A deep remembrance of the wisdom that lies within me has occurred and a solid foundation of trust and faith has formed that gives me so much strength and courage. I have a settled feeling of knowing and a deep trust in backing myself and a feeling of being unmovable in that.

My skill level of self-mastery, alchemy, energy protection and energy reading has skyrocketed. I love the fact that I know that I can energetically protect myself, my family and my home, one hundred percent. Nothing can mess with us energetically without meeting my light and my kick-ass support crew, who I am blessed to have working with me.

Another one of the major key amplifications and gifts that has been revealed since the beginning of my training with Sentaura is my capacity to understand and hold compassion for our human consciousness and behaviour. This has expanded tenfold. I can see and feel way beyond the surface layers. This enables me to understand beliefs and societal systems easily and I seem to be able to deconstruct and simplify these matrixes.

To explain it pictorially, it is like having a ball of wire wool in front of me and I can unravel it with minimal effort and see straight into the core to the actual cause. This has been incredibly helpful in working as a healer and helps me in my wider life with navigating parenting, relationships and world happenings.

Over the course of centuries, I definitely feel that the understanding, ideas, concepts and societal beliefs have been way over complicated, secretive, deemed unreachable or privileged. This is a big subject, but I shall pick out the relevant pieces.

We have been completely disempowered. Beliefs that psychic abilities, creation, manifesting, transmutation, and many other forms of magic are limited to the 'chosen' with 'special' gifts.

These gifts are incredibly special, but we ALL have them! A happy and fulfilled life where we are responsible for our outcomes is way more simple, reachable and achievable than we have ever been led to believe. Consider for a moment, what do you believe you are capable of? Where does this belief originate? Is it true? Is your heart whispering it or is it what you have been told or led to believe about yourself?

I believe that if each individual, around the entire planet had a much more enlightened level of understanding, compassion and love for themselves, their surrounding community and our planet, we would have a very different world. Sentaura is definitely here to help create this in the hearts of humanity and so much more.

Another one of my gifts that was activated by Sentaura and was a major shift for me, is that I can now fully differentiate between feelings and energy belonging to me or feelings and energy that is coming from the collective. Until I learnt how to tell the difference things were very tricky.

Quite often I would question: "Why am I feeling like this?" Because it just wasn't making sense and it would often leave me feeling uncertain and wobbly. Especially with the turmoil that we've been experiencing with the oppression and loss of our freedoms via ridiculous government rules of late.

I personally think it is a skill everyone would benefit from learning, and it would make a massive difference to people's mental health and well-being. It would also naturally raise the consciousness of humanity by default. It has certainly raised mine and the consciousness of my family because of my expanded awareness.

Being an empath, I have always had the gift of being able to see others' perspectives. Sentaura has amplified this gift and with it comes a magnified sense of 'seeing'. The ability to be able to zoom out for a wider perspective of situations is especially important in the times that we live in.

With so much conflicting information, division, many sources of opinions and many nervous systems stuck in the fight or flight response, which is the sympathetic nervous system, it is easy to get rattled or to fall into overwhelm over the small and big things that happen to us.

Being able to step away and master our own energy is critical to our survival and a skill set that would benefit all of humanity if we role model it and teach it to our children.

Self-doubt has also always played a massive part in me not knowing and accepting my full ability as a channel of wisdom, healing, and connection to the divine and oneness of all that is.

I'll be honest, self-doubt sometimes still creeps in and it always will. I am fantastically human after all even though I have cleared an awful lot of the debris away. I think one of the major idiosyncratic aspects of being a human is to figure out how we can get out of our own way.

How can we open up our channels and the parts of the brain we do not use, to the infinite limitless potential of creation, connection and harmony that is available to us? It is just sitting there waiting for us to be ready.

Through Sentaura remembrance and acknowledgement of the wisdom that lies within me has been reawakened, reignited, and stabilised into solid foundations and fully grounded within my being. I feel so gloriously centred and empowered in who I am and what I am here to do. I feel completely unshakable.

Do not get me wrong, I am always learning and rediscovering. It is a lifelong process, that is for sure, and I build, expand, test out and evolve on my firm yet flexible foundations. I didn't have this sense of confidence prior to Sentaura. I would have moments of groundedness but a lot of the time I felt like I was floating like a cork, bobbing with no anchor to stabilise me, from one thing to another.

I was constantly wondering who I truly was and why I was really here. Of course, being a double Virgo I made this way more complicated than it needed to be. That is something I truly love about Sentaura, it strips away the bullshit, fluffiness, drama, untruths and safety of the ego. There is no space to hide until really all that is left is your bare bones, exposed in all of their glory, shining bright.

And Now to Close This Magical Portal

Many moons ago our magic was robbed from us. Our unique special spark and power was taken, and we allowed it to be. We chose to give away our power and fill the void with layer upon layer of lies, misbeliefs, trauma, separation, disconnectedness, guilt, shame, blame, false beliefs, materialism, dissociation of self, fear of the darkness and shadow. Imposed by leaders through power, greed and control. All of this was placed in the space where our light once was.

The modern-day human is a shell of its true potential, capability and capacity. We have filled ourselves with so much heaviness, non-truths, false love and consumerism. It is time to differentiate what is actually for us, lights us up and brings us joy. It is time to let go of fear and what does not serve us anymore. If it is fear-based, it is not love.

The time has come to clear away the centuries of old debris, out-of-date behavioural patterns and bullshit his-story that is not our own. It is time to smash away the spoon that has been feeding humanity this false reality, that only serves itself.

Claim back your magic light that IS you. Take back your impeccable divine sovereignty. Embody your truth, love, freedom, joy, pleasure and creativity. Love what you do and do what you love. It is all possible. Just see what you can really do and BE!!

Thank you, dear soul, for taking the time to sit and read the glimpse of my Sentaura journey. I hope it leaves you inspired, curious, empowered, uplifted and most of all gifts you the permission slip to live and BE everything that you literally 'one of a kind' can BE.

My eternal infinite gratitude and love to Natali for her impeccable authenticity, determination, incredible teachings, epic support and space holding, soul SiStar love and amazing hugs. Also, so much kudos, respect and appreciation to Natali for getting completely out of her own way, taking that massive leap of faith, trusting and bringing this phenomenal gift that is Sentaura to our hearts, our beloved planet and humanity. Thank you.

A massive thank you to my Sentaura SiStars for their heartfelt love, connection, wisdom, support, tears, giggles and kickass magic! Finally, a deep soul heart thank you to the Divine, The Seraphim Creation Angels and all light energies that protect, guide and bless us every day.

I shall leave you with much love and a blessing that is here on my wall. Author unknown.

"May your troubles be less, and your blessings be more and nothing but happiness come through your door. Put family first, love life every day and may nothing but joy ever come your way".

GEORGINA CURNOW

ABOUT THE AUTHOR

Georgina is a conscious heart leader, the visionary creator of Elegant Empowerment and is here to ignite self-empowerment, mastery and remembrance bringing light, love and joy back to your heart and to humanity. She is a certified Sentaura Healing Practitioner and Cosmic Alchemist of Light, Crystal Healer, Empowerment Mentor, Ceremonial Cacao and Breathwork Facilitator.

Her offerings are an amalgamation of her life loves, heart whispers and soul callings, blended together. Her passions are in teaching, healing and empowering women to realise their complete worth, creativity, joy and magic.

Georgina works holistically, guiding clients back to their hearts, soul essence and centre point, through expansive wisdom, compassion and alchemy helping them to navigate the journey back into divine sovereignty.

Georgina is Cornish and lives in New Zealand. She is a wife and mother blessed with two Cornish-kiwi children.

Website:
http://www.elegantempowerment.co.nz/

Facebook:
https://www.facebook.com/Beautifuladie

Instagram:
https://www.instagram.com/elegantempowerment9/

FINDING MY VOICE AND MY TRUTH

SHARLENE ELLIS

3

I stood rigid, terrified, and giant tears rolled down my face. A tiny voice reached out to the only adult in the room, "no I don't want to be seen" "I am so afraid of being seen" "please don't make me do this".

Natali kept saying "it's ok, I know" and gently held space for my inner little girl to be heard. Eventually with every inch of bravery, I allowed myself to open, to feel this raw lost emotion and to try to understand it. Why did I become paralysed in fear anytime I contemplated speaking out loud, why did I not want to share my gifts, talents and deep wisdom with the world, or even my own friends and family? A part of me felt completely closed off, wanting to stay in the security and comfort of a quiet life, yet part of me really wanted to step out.

My inner child trembled, and tantrumed, and closed off. She was a stubborn wee thing, determined to hide and keep herself safe. Surely stepping out would bring her unwanted attention, judgment and ridicule. Stepping out would have the 'bad people' notice her and she might be beaten or yelled at, or worse. Her memories of human nature were not kind.

Keeping quiet as a child kept me safe, and not sharing my insights with people kept me under the radar. Going unnoticed became a superpower, and I developed a chameleon ability of either blending in or just leaving a social gathering when it got too much. No one could know how 'strange' I was, how out of place in this world I felt, if I just stayed safe, quiet, normal and boring. I had no idea people did notice me, and by disappearing I hurt my friend's feelings.

That day through the power of Sentaura, Natali and I worked together to calm my inner child, surround her with universal love, and to remove the darkness that had attached itself to her, keeping her locked away and feeding on my fear. I remember feeling incredibly nauseous and emotional but sticking with it.

Allowing myself to feel was the only way to release it. It was important to release it because being afraid of speaking up no longer served me in the life I wanted to lead.

I could not understand why the fear was so strong in me, until I released a past life where I was stalked and killed by someone I never met. I let go of layers of fear of other people, abandonment, and unhelpful stories around perfectionism.

These were all massive in their own right—complementing each other to reveal a person who did not want to be seen on a public stage, or even guide a crowd of forty people through meditation. Facing the public in this way was a huge trigger for me and the catalyst for these feelings bubbling up in the first place.

In shamanic teachings you would say I called back pieces of my own soul, and I returned pieces of other people's souls that were caught within the trauma I had suffered as a child. It was palpable and I could feel the difference, and suddenly speaking up wasn't such an issue, in fact, it felt like it had never been a problem.

I nourished my inner child, welcoming her into the space within my heart, allowing her to rest. I asked her what she needed in order to be seen and heard. That was an interesting question when the whole session was around being seen! But she spoke up, she was brave and sassy. She told me she wanted to dance. She wanted animals to love. She wanted to play.

Three days later, nervous, but not terrified, I held space for forty people and guided them from the heart through meditation. It went really well. Nobody said I shouldn't be doing it the way I was doing it—nobody judged me or even noticed my trembling voice. People liked what I had to share and had their own special moments connecting with the plant kingdom as I guided them through journeying with the powerful Kanuka tree. A Sentaura Practitioner was born.

Listening To the Guidance from My Soul

It took me a while to say yes to the Sentaura Practitioner training but I'm so glad I did. I felt a strong pull towards it, and it kept coming across my path, so eventually I asked my guides if I should do the training. I always asked them about any big decisions, the last business training I asked about they said I would achieve my goals with or without it, so I didn't pursue that. I asked the same question about this Sentaura Training, "Do I need to do this training? Will I achieve my soul calling without this course?" My answer was, "yes you will, over many lifetimes" "Wait, what? How long will it take me?"

I pulled some oracle cards questioning whether to do this work and I got 'healer of the ages' which is a picture of Jesus, and I received other cards with Archangel Metatron, Archangel Michael and Archangel Raphael. I had no idea of the real impact these Angels would have on my life but wow, it felt supportive and the Sentaura training felt like it was something I definitely needed to do.

I already had a history of being a healer for two years, a naturopath and a herbalist for nearly twenty years. I stepped onto my path as a Healer when I was attuned to Reiki and started working with the intense healing flowing from my hands. My Reiki Master said I held so much light, that healing was my destiny, and I had likely been a healer in past lives. I had an intense knowing that the light that came through me when doing healing was something I was yet to learn about. Friends and teachers started commenting "there is so much light around you" "your healing is powerful". My teacher started doing swaps with me and each time she would comment she felt several people working on her when receiving healing from me.

When Covid hit New Zealand and we went into lockdown for six weeks I started working with a Shaman online—she taught meditation, channelling, symbolism and how to understand my psychic ability. Her teachings put me on the right track and helped me understand my own energy in a way that felt perfect for me.

What I needed however was more confidence, and a deeper understanding of ways in which to use my energy healing abilities. Working with Natali and Sentaura has given me all of that and so much more. My energy healing abilities and confidence have increased, and my abilities aren't limited to other people, I also send healing to the Earth, plants, animals and so much more. I am so thankful for Natali's gentle guidance, Sentaura and the Seraphim.

How Sentaura Changed My Life for Good

During my pre-initiation session with Natali which gets your body ready to receive the initiations and higher frequency of Sentaura, I had my first "wow" moment. I felt an energy move up my legs, and Natali said, "Mother Gaia has just come in so strongly for you". It felt exciting that Mother Gaia wanted to work with me, and I began to see visions of times past where I had worked with the rhythms of the Earth—the ebb and flow of the tide, the cyclical motions of the seasons.

I saw myself with my hands in the dirt, carving symbols into cave walls, picking armloads of golden sunflowers, and walking through ancient forests speaking with the trees, the rivers, the mountains and so much more. I felt both elated and a sense of coming home.

The Sentaura Program officially kicked off and Natali guided us through the first initiation. My experience of this initiation with my other soul sisters in the group was sun-drenched, light-filled, a deliverance of beauty, joy and love.

Honestly, I was floored, it felt so angelic. I felt at one with the sun, radiating light. I felt completely blissed out and didn't remember much else other than feelings of inclusivity, of knowing I was in the right place, of worlds opening, beings wanting to connect—

not that I realised what that was until later—and just plain joy and acceptance. I'm sure these are feelings everyone craves.

During another initiation, we were all gifted the Sentaura Sword of Freedom™ and I felt it so deeply in my whole being. This was gifted as a tool to use anytime I needed to cut away the 'crap', to cut cords or attachments to things that were not healthy, to cleanse auras, and cut things away from places they didn't need to be.

As always, I asked for it to happen as long it was for the highest greatest good of all involved. Each initiation activated a deep remembrance within me and somehow, I had an innate knowing of how to work with each gift and the channelled wisdom that was shared by Natali. The initiations unlocked our dormant key codes and the wisdom of our souls. Using the gifts and tools which were activated through each initiation made my healing work more powerful, and so much quicker.

I was able to efficiently 'cut through' dense layers in only one Sentaura healing session. Previously it would require me to do several Reiki sessions over a year to obtain a similar result. Sentaura was working much quicker, and it was liberating.

By week two and three I was in a lot of physical pain. My head, shoulders and arms were all super tight, and I was in agony. I wondered if it was resistance coming up because my body was being upgraded to hold more Sentaura Cosmic Light and whether my body could handle it.

I admit, it scared me, and I went through all the emotions of why was I doing this, was I good enough? Could I physically handle this? Natali assured me I could.

I began to bring awareness to this pain and decided not to shrug it off, "as per usual Sharlene". I became aware that the pain originated right between my shoulder blades. Suddenly, Jesus was with me, showing me that my body was literally being rebuilt. He worked like a carpenter on the structure of my physical arms, shoulders, and upper body.

Jesus told me that my arms needed to be able to channel more healing light, and that my healing ability would be upgraded. He showed me how I place my hands on others and the stunning, powerful light that emitted from my hands. I was totally blown away.

Toward the end of this rebuilding session, I saw a giant set of feathery wings form behind me and moved my arms to experience them. The physical pain I experienced was the energetic growing of my wings.

Healing My Ancestral Line

Around the same time, I became aware of some ancestral trauma that needed healing - my ancestors coming in closer and closer. Holding me, needing me.

I channelled the following message.

"Our bloodline has been suppressed:

The mother has been ignored, beaten, raped,

and treated second class or of no class at all.

She's had to stand up for herself as no one else does.

The men in this line were very dark, it's a line of the abused and abusers.

The mothers, the women, hold a victim mentality.

They believe "but I love him so much and would do anything to keep him happy".

While "he" is the ultimate manipulator, she is too as she tries to SURVIVE"

I had goosebumps, finally understanding that our feminine line did what they thought was for the best, each generation teaching the next, to keep themselves and their family safe. She made herself small, she did what she thought the masculine liked, she followed his lead, she did not dare to shine her own light in front of him. It was sobering to see so many generations suffer, and I knew it had to stop with me.

I was guided to heal the feminine line first, to help her find herself, see her strength, her mana, her worth, her fortitude. Through healing the feminine line first, the masculine line would follow.

My entire female ancestral line was leaning in to help me do the inner work. They encouraged me and celebrated with me. I wasn't doing this just for myself, I would do it for my own children and their children's children. This abusive pattern which was still strong in my own childhood was going to STOP NOW.

With the loving frequency of Sentaura to help me we collapsed timelines, worked through the mindset of being unworthy, broke free of chains connecting us to ancestral mindsets and let all that shit go, because it wasn't mine.

This release hit me hard and I felt a little lost afterward. I felt as if the pieces of me that I released were the pieces that held me together. I felt uncomfortable like I needed to wear-in my new skin. What released was not only my lifetime long mindsets, but that of my ancestors as well. I knew not to call those pieces back, they were no longer for my highest greatest good but how could I fill the hole that was left?

I got a pen and paper and made a list. A list of all the things I wanted for my life. Abundance, joy, fun, love, and I consulted little Sharlene (my inner child) to ask her what she wanted.

She wanted to be heard. She wanted to stomp her feet on the Earth, she wanted magic. She created a ritual.

IGNITE YOUR FIRE - *A Ceremony to Bring in The New*

Start with giving yourself two hours alone, yes it can be done quicker, but part of the ritual is to give time to YOURSELF and YOUR needs alone. If you think you can't commit to two hours, then you probably need this more than you can imagine.

We will start by pampering our feet. An Epsom salt bath, a massage, moisturizer, paint toenails and adorn the feet. I like to use flowers in my foot bath and henna to paint. Let's get creative and artistic!

Now it's time to put on some music, something that makes you happy. It is so much fun to wear something flowy. I wore a long red dress, but you can wear what makes you feel good.

If you feel called to, you can write the things you want to call in on a piece of paper and burn it in the fire when you are done.

Light a candle to do this or go outside and light the outside fire to dance around so you can call in the Fire element. This is the action element.

Say these words: "I call in FIRE". Feel the energy of it move through your body warming every part from your feet to head and paying particular attention to any spot that is yearning for release, for the alchemy of the fire, or any areas which are in pain.

Then say these words: "I call in PASSION". Again, feel it in every part of your body. Your feet up to the head and really embody that feeling of passion and repeat this process with any feeling you desire to call in.

I call in BEAUTY

I call in LOVE

I call in GRATITUDE

I call in JOY

I call in FREEDOM

I call in (INSERT YOUR OWN)

Dance it out

Stomp those beautiful feet into the ground and then go forth and conquer your dreams.

When something is released, you need to bring in the new, to create direction and flow. It also stops you unconsciously calling back the things you released. Through setting intentions, making wishes or goals, and strengthening the belief in yourself you can create all the things you wish to be.

The Emotional Pain Body and Sentaura Royal Creator Key Code of Joy ™

During this initiation we explored the different layers of the human aura, particularly concentrating on the emotional pain body. Working with the emotional pain body was surreal.

Natali guided us to enter a crystalline pool of water and release our pain. It was all soft and languid like I was swimming at twilight. I felt all the pain, yet none of the pain. At times there was a lot of water energy moving through me and it felt heavy.

When Natali said during the initiation that we may feel water on our skin, like a light sweat, I felt like I released gushes of water. It was pouring from my aura and another gush released from my sacral area and between my legs.

Although some of the water was deep and heavy to move through, it was pristine, crisp and cool. I felt like I released a lot of pain, both emotional and physical into the water. Afterward, I stepped out of the water all cleansed and sparkly.

During this initiation, I received the Sentaura Key Code of Joy floating down from the cosmos and into the palm of my hands and then out onto each finger pad. I put my two hands out in front of me and saw the Code of Joy inside a ball of energy in between my hands. I was able to stretch it and move it to be the size I wanted and even place it over a complete person lying on the massage table to envelop them in the joy code.

This is one of my favourite Sentaura codes. Whenever I work with this code it leaves me with a huge grin on my face, my eyes sparkle, and I often find myself giggling. It is truly a beautiful code and energy to work with.

Near the end of the initiation, my ancestors appeared with a golden gift in their hands. They held an 'energetic' thyroid and placed it in my throat chakra. This was a life-changing gift, and I wept in gratitude.

I knew my thyroid was a little underactive, but it never showed on tests. A low thyroid brings symptoms of low energy and depression or no joy in life. After that I felt my energy levels were lifted and better controlled, I started to release weight, and my mood definitely improved.

The Sentaura Code of Joy™ reminds me that we are all powerful beings, and that having fun is so important.

Having this code and its energy embodied has continued to expand the potency of my work. I see this code in everyday life, or in various things, not just during healing sessions with people. It comes through when I am making herbal medicines, undoubtedly as part of my creation process but also in the energy of the plants.

During a meditation to connect with the Kanuka Tree, I could see and feel the joy code in the plant and found myself smiling from ear to ear. I met the spirit of the Kanuka Tree—an older man with his grey hair in a ponytail. He had a casual demeanour, rolled a cigarette joint and laughed, telling me that the smoke of the Kanuka was powerful medicine. His eyes were sparkling with joy.

He told me Kanuka is a potent cleanser of the body and space, and it can be used in a similar way to how we use white sage from America. He told me to burn it to create smoke in a home that needs more joy and upliftment. Kanuka is to be used after saging, as sage removes the negative and Kanuka brings in the positive.

Healing In the Moment

Normal life as a mother continues. We had a birthday party to go to, but my little guy wasn't feeling well and was dry retching from feeling nauseous. He can get a little separation anxiety and was missing his sister who was away at camp. He just wanted cuddles with me, so I did some healing on him during our cuddles. I started with his feet which seemed to calm him down then moved to his head and crown chakra.

It looked like he was almost asleep, but his head still felt busy and heavy. I pictured him dropping the emotional pain in his body and him stepping into a pool of water, just like Natali guided us to when working with our own emotional pain bodies. I asked to release any pain, emotions and attachments not for his highest good and asked for it to be transmuted by the Angels.

I helped to clear his crown chakra. It felt like he received his energy from the earth and from me and his sister, not really making or connecting with his own Source and universal love. I opened his crown chakra a little to receive his own energy so he could stand in his own power and hopefully not be so needy of others. Two hours later he was the life of the party running around and eating party food. He wasn't clingy at all. Kids are often easy to work with and receive healing even quicker than adults as they are so open to healing.

Healing My Heart

Working with Sentaura is so interesting, often when I take a moment to rest, I will receive my own healing and insights. This particular day, a powerful healing energy entered my awareness. I felt completely calm, peaceful and gently joyful. Then I saw him—Archangel Raphael. He was holding a heart in his hands, and I knew it was my heart beating peacefully as he tended to its wounds, its pain and past life trauma. I lay still and bathed in His presence, unbelievably grateful for a moment of peace.

These words came to me: "This heart has many scars; many traumas have obscured its light. It has been burnt at the stake, it has been suppressed, it has energetically left the body several times. It is a beautiful heart and capable of holding so much light and enough love to heal itself and others".

Many times during my Sentaura journey, I felt the need to hold the space where my heart is, or should be, and simply send it healing. It feels powerful, incredibly nourishing, and like I am working on many layers of my heart, over many lifetimes.

I get a lot of visions too, in which I see the trauma that is ready to be released. In this lifetime I find myself in a place of polar opposites, either fully activated beyond belief and insanely sensitive, or in complete disconnect. Allowing myself to receive love has always been difficult and trusting that it is real has been harder. I could feel all the healing helping with that, slowly cracking HER open to receive back all I can be.

One morning after sending healing to my heart the night before, I woke to an image of my ex holding my heart in his hands and giving it back to me. I was angry. I realised I had given it to him when we were together, in the hope that he would love me.

I can see now that it was my wounded inner child desperately wanting to be loved and I was shown a pattern. It was not the first time I had given away my heart, it started as a child, with my father, wanting him to love me.

The thought of me giving my heart away made me very sad. My heart is for me, she is for my body to continue living, she is for self-love and for loving others and I can do that much better when she is a part of me—I do not ever have to give her away. It felt like a raw open wound. I needed to be kinder to myself, I didn't know any better back then.

I had to heal many past lives where my heart was broken, abused or neglected. I had to have help, this stuff was big and emotional. Working with Natali I healed so much of this, and she would always pick up on my heart energy.

She could see how my past life experiences affected the energy of my heart and the connection with my soul light. She told me I had a 'clamp' around my heart, a feeling of not being safe, it felt very closed, it was burnt in a past life and so much more.

When my heart is activated, I feel extreme joy flowing through me. The colours in the world are more vibrant and beautiful, and I am filled with wonder, especially connected to nature and all its beauty. I talk to the trees, the fairies, the whales, and it all fills my heart with so much joy and emotion.

We are able to communicate with these beings when we radiate joy from the heart because the heart opens the gateway for universal communication and so love is felt by all.

Delving into the Akashic Records

The Sentaura Akashic Records Creator Key Code is simply stunning!

This initiation was so beautiful, and I received it with ease. I felt as if I've been working in the Akashic records for some time. I had past lives come through often in healing sessions with clients, usually outlining why someone is struggling with particular feelings at the time due to the experiences of a past life. I didn't realise the impact of this initiation and how it amplified my abilities until I did a healing for a client and got to bask in the amazingness of it.

The layers of past lives revealed to me during this healing were so intense. I saw my client's heart in front of me, and then the akashic records opened like a book, each page revealing a different life story where her heart was hurt in some way.

She was born with an enlarged heart and died young, she was poisoned with something that affected the beating of her heart, she sat on the throne as a princess but was killed by an arrow to the heart. I could see it all and could barely keep up, the visions were coming so fast.

I had to write shorthand! Everything I was shown was coming up to be released and timelines collapsed so that she could move on with a heart free of fear.

The akashic record code can also be applied to the land, and in doing so it brings up visions of what has happened there in the past and what the land needs to be healed.

Healing The Land with Sentaura

I had a client approach me having problems with 'spirits' or bad vibes in her house and on her land. She asked a local Māori healer to bless the land, but the person was unwell and was not able to make the appointment. Although I couldn't go to her property in person, as she was in the South Island of New Zealand and I was in the North Island, I offered to tune in and see what I could see. Maybe it could help, it certainly couldn't hurt while she waited for the land to be blessed.

I asked Sentaura for help, and there was an energy of urgency around me like it was already powered up and ready to work. I was guided to move outside my house, and to draw a circle around me with salt before proceeding. Although we are extremely protected with Sentaura, this felt like another layer, building up the protection for what was to be an enormous process. Doing it outside connected me with the land. I have previously done Earth healing but during this session my visions came through so clear and vibrant, I honestly felt like I was standing on her land, and I wondered if she could feel me there.

I opened my eyes for a moment and saw I had various animals join me for this healing. First a family of Tui came and sat in their usual spot in my bottle brush tree. Then a black cat walked down the driveway, a kingfisher settled on the neighbours' tree, plus ducks, seagulls and a white cat all came into my healing space. I was blessed with animals and although this may seem normal, there weren't that many animals around my home before. I thanked them all for their help.

I set my intention to look around at my client's land and to send it healing. I asked my guides and her guides of the highest light to help us. The Seraphim joined me as they often do when working with the Sentaura energy, but this time I could sense six of them! They immediately directed me to work beneath the land creating a crystal grid.

I had never done anything like that before. The energy of Sentaura was pulsing through my body, the heat in my hands was immense and gently they guided me on what to do. Together we pushed giant white and black crystals into the land energetically and created a pattern that seemed to pull the energy together rather than it being scattered in all directions with no real flow.

I thanked them deeply for their help and then my attention went to the chicken coop, where I met with a 'lost soul'. This person had passed suddenly from loss of blood and had not been able to cross over yet.

He was fearful and I recognised the energy of abandonment within him. He had died alone. Next, I saw a vicious wolf and although I did not feel afraid, I was very thankful for the protection I had set up around my energy.

He felt angry and it felt like he would hurt me, but underneath it all he too was suffering, and I could see the code of abandonment within him too. I realised there was a pattern of abandonment I needed to release, and I could see how the fear code of abandonment was also reflected in my client and her land.

The wolf was attached to my client from a past life where she had been an old man and died because he broke his collarbone in a fall and was unable to get himself up. He died all alone because no one came to help.

Because of this experience my client incarnated into this life holding the code of abandonment in her cell memory. The Wolf had been his pet and when he died the wolf was sad and abandoned. So, the abandonment code needed to be healed in her past life, this life, in the wolf, with the lost soul, and in her land.

By acknowledging and removing the abandonment code the wolf calmed down very quickly and promised to protect and look after my client, like a good dog would. He said she could ask him to patrol the house each night and keep guard.

I sent the land healing and healing to my client. I could sense her root chakra, which wasn't functioning very well, and is representative of her connection with the land. By healing it I hoped to connect her back to her land, and her own power and to break the cycle of 'abandonment' which was feeding the fear on the land and within my client.

During the healing and clearing, the guardians of her land came forward. They wanted to meet with her, so I asked her to talk to them, respect the land, treat it like you would a friend. The session was epic, and she said the energy of the land felt way better. After this an issue arose with her water supply, but I personally feel that needed to happen in order for it to be properly fixed.

A few months later she got an amazing offer on her property as someone came to look at it before it was even for sale and made her an offer she couldn't refuse. The buyer loved the feel of the place.

The Orion Initiation

Six months into the Sentaura program and I am feeling pretty unstoppable, amazing and excited to be learning more.

This initiation sat me on my butt in surprise and pain. As Natali led us through the initiation, I could feel deep seated pain in my body rise to be released. It was so intense that I cried out and Natali suggested I should lie down in the middle of the circle and bathe in the light coming into my body.

I could feel my rib cage expanding to hold the light and it hurt. I wanted to fall into the foetal position and weep, instead I opened my eyes and looked up at the woman surrounding me, each deep in their own initiation process and each holding space for me with so much care and love that it helped me to feel strong.

What happened that day blew my mind. During the initiation Natali transmitted a frequency and message from the Orion Star Beings, our cosmic family.

For the first time in my life, I understood there were beings from other planets and stars that were around us, and that they could help us if we asked.

The frequency of Sentaura continued to work with us after the initiation and I had an epic experience during a dance yoga class. I went into deep meditation during movement and found myself buried underneath the ground, in a tunnel.

I realized I was inside a tunnel that was inside a pyramid. I didn't know it at the time, but a quick 'google' later revealed that people had been put in tunnels in pyramids as human sacrifices in the past. That hit me like a tonne of bricks—I had been a human sacrifice.

Through meditation and connection with my higher self I was told that I was sacrificed because I had an ability to communicate with beings from other planets. I was seen as different, to be feared, so they used me as a sacrifice. And because of this I shut down my ability to communicate with or even acknowledge other beings. I felt that it was not safe for me to communicate with them. In my vision I saw myself go 'poof' replaced by skull and crossbones, my life had ended.

The next minute, I was back in the tunnel, I could feel my arms pinned down to my sides and I wiggled and wiggled, moving inch by inch to finally reach the surface and be free. The relief and disbelief when I reached the surface filled me with bliss. I reached my arms out to their full capacity and smiled to see big blue moth wings attached to my arms. I had hatched out of the ground, born anew with my abilities restored. The wings were attached to my throat, my communication centre, and of the brightest blue.

Later that week, I finally joined an online healing group that I had been told about but never really felt the urge to join. It was run by the father of a client of mine, he is an energy healer, and he took us on a meditation journey. We journeyed energetically to Arcturus, a star near Earth. I could say so much about these journeys as they have always been mind-blowing and helped me to get closer to the energy of universal love, which is amazing.

I had new visions, where I worked with crystals, and I saw my future, guiding people along ancient paths of earth healing, uncovering alien artifacts, and places of healing and working with those places to create potent healing on Earth and for Earth's people.

All these things only happened after my Sentaura Orion Initiation. I would have not had the courage to join the group if it wasn't for Sentaura. I had a lot of fear to clear around connecting and communicating with other beings, planets and civilizations.

I noticed during these visioning journeys I also spent a lot of time with the Sun and the Moon. I would bask in their energy.

I have always had a beautiful connection to planet Earth. I love Her and there is nothing better than my bare feet on the ground, soaking up the energy and connecting with Her, sending Her my love and receiving Hers. During Sentaura Earth healing sessions, I started noticing the other planets within our solar system entering the healing circle and offering their healing energy.

One time the bright yellow energy of Mercury entered, looking like power lines and electricity (our local power company is called Mercury so I believe it was my guides trying to tell me what was bringing the energy into our session).

I told my Sentaura sisters, "I think the planet Mercury wants to join us" and they agreed, they felt it too. Upon researching it, I found out that Mercury was in pretty close proximity to Earth at the time.

A similar thing happened with Jupiter, during a shamanic meditation to meet with my guides. I was greeted on the beach by six small Jupiterians. They were literally little green beings, and they moved simply through intention. They hugged me and told me to set my heart intention to go to Jupiter, next minute, we were there. We were floating through the atmosphere and my human body waited to hit the ground. They laughed and told me: "there is no "ground" no "solid" on Jupiter, we simply exist in the ether".

They told me to think of anything and I could immediately manifest it. I wanted something solid beneath me, so I visualised a sun lounger and a cocktail, next minute I had both. Suspended in the atmosphere of Jupiter I relaxed on a sun lounger and sipped on a coconut cocktail. My Jupiterian friends laughed and laughed with so much joy and pleasure. We didn't 'speak' the same language but through our heart and soul connection we fully understood each other, and the purity of our giggles is something I will always remember.

This connection with the Jupiterians was to remind me of the gift I had inside to manifest anything I needed and to manifest with pure joy because the energy of joy amplifies everything. They reminded me to use the power of my heart to communicate with anyone, and to communicate my dreams.

In the beginning of our Sentaura journey I made a list with my children of all the things we wanted our dream house to be. The kids wanted a bigger space.

They wanted a big lounge, bigger bedrooms and storage space like a garage. We wanted a clinic room for me to work from, a garden or space to create a garden and a beach view. By the time I finished the Sentaura program we achieved all those goals plus it is a house that my family was able to buy so we aren't renting from a landlord anymore.

I find it important to set the intention and to 'manifest' my dreams often, and I like to set reminders, to be present and to feel gratitude for what I already have.

Unicorns and Angels

The daughter of my client told me her mum needs regular healing, and that she loves unicorns and angels. She was going to send her to me as she felt I would be a good match.

Love is a beautiful thing, as I connected to my client's energy the unicorns and angels were already around her. I saw her placed inside a temple teaching other healers. The angelic beings were around her. It was as if she was one of them, and the unicorns responded to her with love. It was beautiful to see.

Through the power of Sentaura and the unicorns I was shown something they called the 'rainbow highway'. They told me it is the connection between the high heart chakra and the throat chakra. I was shown how to open that 'highway' in my client. It was something that has been closed off due to modern life, and suppression of our voices. The rainbow highway is about speaking and living your true life purpose. It is about speaking from the heart, and just being you, as you are meant to be from a soul perspective.

How beautiful is that! I thanked Sentaura and the unicorns for their gift and insight. I went on to use that technique in some of my other clients as well and it is something that is opening up in many of us.

During our session I also had a giant fluffed up Tui bird come into the room as a guide for my client. The Tui, Māori believe, has two voice boxes, one that speaks or sings what we can hear, and one that can be heard in the spirit realm. He is a beautiful black bird representing the West directionally in shamanism. He came through to help with the healing on her throat chakra and to help her use her voice.

My Experience with Sentaura Distance Healing

Some of my healing clients are based overseas and I worked with them prior to joining Sentaura, during, and after the seven-month program. As I was progressing through the Sentaura program it felt as if each client healing becoming more expansive, revealing more layers than the one before. Sentaura is a very exciting energy to work with. I never knew what would come through for the client or what we would be focusing on, but it was always spot on and exactly what my clients needed.

I started the healing session for Miss J by burning sage to cleanse myself and my room. I asked her guides and of course the Seraphim and Sentaura to help us, and guide us to what needed to be healed.

I pictured her in front of me on the massage table, focusing on her body and for the first time ever I was shown golden lines in the body—similar to Meridian lines but they were able to move around, and highlight different areas in the body that needed healing. One golden line went from her brain down to the small of her back and I received the words "HPA axis".

I love how Sentaura and our guides work with your level of knowledge. It might be explained to others differently, but because of my work as a naturopath I knew all about the HPA axis (Hypothalamus, Pituitary, Adrenal Axis).

This hormonal feedback system can get out of balance, usually from a traumatic event, but also the modern world of stress, the fast pace of life, and the food we eat can contribute. It can present as chronic stress, depression, anxiety, low energy, and poor blood sugar balance to name a few symptoms.

I worked to calm her system, sending it healing from my hands. I zoomed in on the golden lines and realised they were lines of code.

I hadn't yet studied to be a Sacred Architect, but Natali got all excited, saying I was being gifted something she would be teaching in her new Sacred Architect course.

The Seraphim showed me how to use my sword of freedom to 'cut out' the codes that were causing problems or misfiring and to leave the healthy ones. It was like snipping a gene out of a DNA sequence and then reattaching the strand so it could work correctly. Sometimes there was a specific message in the code to be understood.

Once again, I saw the fear code of abandonment. It was lodged in part of her brain and was impeding her brain function—all her thoughts were filtered through this fear of abandonment. No wonder she was under constant stress.

I was shown a past life where she was buried alive and the abandonment code presented itself not only as mistrust of people, but as a deep abandonment she felt from the Earth itself because the Earth had covered her up and allowed her to die.

She confirmed, she didn't naturally feel a connection with and to the Earth in ways she thought she should when doing meditations, and that she felt quite removed from it. After this session she vowed to get out in nature more and reconnect with the Earth.

I had another client with a 'swollen' code on her arm. My guides told me it was caused by a vaccination injury to the arm that had changed her DNA coding. I could see a normal strand of DNA, but one part was more swollen and bigger than the rest. I knew that it no longer worked the way it should and due to the damage, the connections between the whole strand were short circuiting. This felt significant and I am thankful that I was shown how to use the Sentaura Sword of Freedom Key Code and know I will use it a lot in the coming years.

Natali taught us how to use the 'Sentaura Golden Rod of Balance' and during an initiation we were given 'The Gift of the Rod'. Using this energetic technique, we could bring balance to a person's body. I use it a lot during healing sessions. It is perfect in a world where there is disharmony and chaos and especially used for reharmonizing our energy after Covid and after receiving mandatory vaccinations.

I found that the balance in the body has been really affected by both the virus and the vaccination. I am seeing many of my naturopathic clients coming back with past issues they used to suffer from once they had the vaccination or Covid. It's like we need to start from the beginning with a new health plan to get their health back on track. I've noticed increased inflammation and disharmony in the body especially after vaccination.

Here is an account of one of the healing sessions I did. She is a full-time caregiver.

"The energy of my client looked scattered. It was like electricity was firing and a whole lot of synapses were going off all at once, but they were all heading in different directions and had no place to go. It looked exhausting! She had bruises on her skin, she felt terrible, and her ability to care for others or care about anything was severely affected. I immediately called in the Sentaura Rod of Balance to help the body settle down. I placed my hands at the root chakra and the crown chakra simultaneously and watched as the golden rod floated down and placed itself into my client's body. Once integrated it calmed the body and helped it to regain balance.

How I Work with Sentaura Now

Sentaura created a bridge between understanding and using my gifts. It has taught me how to apply and use my healing ability and to continue to expand it. Natali's guidance and Sentaura's loving frequency showed me my highest path and soul purpose.

My path is still lighting up. I know there is more to unfold but I also enjoy showing others the way, who are at the start of their path. I create healing plans for people which include hands-on healing, distance healing, herbal medicine, and forest walks where they can be fully immersed in the healing from Sentaura, the plants and the Earth. Sentaura always guides me and shows me how to work with you and how to create the best healing plan for you.

Natali has been a wonderful guide, and patient teacher. She is an incredible healer and there have been many times on my own healing journey that I have had to reach out to her for help battling my own challenges. She has helped me to face many things that most people would struggle to look at, many shadows, and each time I went deeper and deeper she never flinched. I simply saw her rise ever greater each time as the wonderful soul she is and battle my shadows with me. She helped me get to the core of my issues whilst slaying the darkness every single time.

I had to dig deep but having support has been invaluable. The more work I do, the more gifts I receive. Clearing unhealthy mindsets makes room for new ideas to flow. This past year has been an incredible journey of ups and downs, shadows and light but most of all Growth. In my healing practice and in myself as a person.

Sentaura has definitely changed my life for the better and learning who I am as a soul and understanding my soul gifts and purpose on earth has brought great security in my life. I am still learning as my healing journey unfolds but now, I look forward to it.

I know there is always more to learn and discover but for now, I'm enjoying the ride.

SHARLENE ELLIS

ABOUT THE AUTHOR

Sharlene Ellis is a Sentaura Healing Practitioner and Alchemist of Light, Shamanic Journey Drum Facilitator and Earth Mother here for the people, plants, animals and our planet. She is a certified Naturopath and Medical Herbalist combining her various skills and talents to create personalised healing sessions depending on your soul's needs.

Her lifelong dedication to healing, natural health and personal transformation helps others to unveil their own gifts and talents and to shine their light and access their happiness and passion for life.

Her soul work includes working with plants and their energetic plant medicine, creating tinctures and providing holistic naturopathic advice, ritual creation for deeper connection, as well as potent Sentaura healing. She also offers herbal foraging walks and weekend retreats alongside her one-on-one consultations.

Sharlene lives in Whangaparaoa in New Zealand with her two children and James the Cat.

Website:
https://www.remedynaturalhealthclinic.co.nz/

Facebook:
https://www.facebook.com/remedynaturalhealthclinic

Instagram:
https://www.instagram.com/remedynaturalhealth

SENTAURA CALLED ME FROM THE DEPTHS OF MY STRUGGLE

KIMBERLEY JADE PIPE

4

I first heard about Sentaura from a friend who was a psychic reader. I was having huge issues in my life and being severely psychically attacked, to the state where I had insomnia and felt like I was losing my mind. During sleep, I would wake with a start, and all I could feel were shadows and darkness around me. When I closed my eyes, I would get debilitating visions and see shadows and felt things I cannot explain attacking me. I had visions of fighting and war and didn't know what to do anymore. I was scared and felt as if I was losing myself.

My nervous system was on edge, and I was beating myself up every moment of every day for things I had done wrong to cause this downfall. This went on for one whole year. I was getting support through various Lightworkers, Councillors, and Doctors and still, I was in an acute state of panic and anxiety.

For the second time in my life, I was in a state of complete burnout and hit rock bottom. I found myself craving the energy and beauty of the Great Barrier Island, and I didn't know how I would get better, but I knew that I had to move back to this island, "where the healers go to heal", as the Waiteha say.

Coming from a past of drug addiction and abuse, I had previously had to move to Great Barrier Island to get myself clean and it worked. After having been clean for six years and touring Europe and the United States DJing Conscious Ecstatic Dance, I pushed myself too hard I stopped eating and developed an eating disorder.

My stomach shrunk so much that I could only eat a tablespoon of food each day. I was super skinny, tired, stressed, and traveling to a different place each day, which left me feeling very ungrounded.

I couldn't eat or sleep or make any decisions and it was terrifying. I would make a decision, then instantly go back on it in fear I had made the wrong one. I was constantly confused and unable to even do the simplest of things, like book flights.

Besides all of this, there has always been an incredible light inside of me—the light of my soul that was calling me HOME. After being in many drug-fuelled situations where I could have easily been very hurt or put in jail, I was always kept safe. I always had support come to me when I needed it—Angels in the disguise of people.

During this difficult time on my travels, I was provided the support I needed, in the way of an amazing American man and a lightworker from Holland. However, I still felt ungrounded, so it wasn't until I went to India on my way home, that I realised just how bad I was. I was caught in so much fear, had intense visions and I couldn't tell a soul what was going on.

I didn't know this at the time, but I came here for a greater purpose, to be the change I wanted to see, to heal people, and because of that, many challenges presented themselves in my life. Many of these obstacles were placed in my way to prevent me from accessing my light and align with my higher soul mission.

I am highly intuitive and during the Sentaura program I uncovered much about myself, my wonderful healing abilities, my innate wisdom, and my true purpose here on Earth. The darkness and attacks I experienced throughout my life were preventing me from being in my power.

I was desperate to get better and every day felt like a struggle. I couldn't do anything I loved confidently and had gone from a confident, happy and driven healer and musician to a depressed, fearful and anxious woman.

After getting back to New Zealand and moving to the Great Barrier Island, I ended up going to see a psych doctor on the island and they put me on anti-psychotic medication. I had tried everything else and for me, this saved me.

Finally, I was able to sleep. Finally, my mind and anxiety started to calm down and I could breathe again and begin to get myself back to some sense of normality. This might not be the solution for everyone, but at the time, it was for me. Being in the Sentaura Program changed everything for me. I realised that working with Sentaura, I no longer needed to be on this medication, and started reducing my doses so now six months later, I'm completely free of any medication.

During an Ecstatic Dance tour in New Zealand, my friend suggested that I connect with Natali for a Sentaura Healing session. She told me that Sentaura would bring me out of the darkness and back into my power. The next day I booked my session and met Natali.

The relief I felt from my first session with Natali was immense. She picked up on exactly what was going on and I felt instantly better. However, I knew it was a big process for me and I needed to keep peeling off the layers to find out what the source of my weakness was.

I received divine guidance that I was to complete the Sentaura Healing Practitioner & Alchemist of Light seven months training and was fully committed to it from the first moment. I simply knew it was for me.

When I find something that really resonates with me and works, I want to learn more about it and share it with my clients. But honestly, at that stage of my life, I wanted to do it for myself. I was in such a fearful place in my life and my business, that I just wanted to be well and somehow, I had this deep knowing that the Sentaura training and working with Natali would bring me out of the depths and back into loving my life.

Little did I know, it would give me so much more—so much more than I could have ever imagined. It gave me back my life and my soul gifts. It unlocked a deep remembrance of my innate abilities and they have flourished like never before.

Now I am helping people with the same issues, helping them get off medication, break free from their shadows, get their lives back on track, and free themselves from addiction, all using Sentaura Healing and combining it with Kinesiology, which I have been practicing for 14 years.

I've had to go to the depths of darkness and back to be able to help those who are struggling.

Being an Empath

Being sensitive and an empath is my superpower. From a young age, I would pick up on everyone's energy and emotions, especially what they were thinking. I could see exactly what was going on for a person, what they needed, and how it was affecting them. I wanted to tell them how I could help or what they needed. This sometimes proved to be very difficult. From the age of seventeen, I started to learn how to differentiate what was mine and what wasn't, but it was a very big journey and with Sentaura it's been much easier to navigate different energies.

I've learned to slow down when I'm tired or run down, as this is when I feel my mind overwhelmed from picking up on everyone's energy and emotions. I find living on my own in nature, away from the hustle and bustle of life brings me peace. Especially with the healing work that I do, I need downtime and stillness.

I would walk into a room and immediately feel if something was off or if someone was not in a good space. I also needed to clear my energy daily, as my etheric field and emotional body could easily get clogged up with other people's energy. During the Sentaura program, I was taught by Natali how to clear my energy effectively and am now teaching others to do the same, which is also part of my life purpose.

Spirit has always been there for me. I felt a connection to God and the Angels from an early age. The most pivotal point in my life, that I can still remember clearly to this day, was when I was five. I was sitting outside on a piece of wood crying. I was crying because I didn't want to be here on Earth.

I didn't understand why I was back on this Earth, living a solitary life. I felt so alone and in so much pain. I was bawling my eyes out when I heard my name: 'Kimberley". I looked up and saw a brilliant white light coming down from the heavens. Yes, just like in the movies. Then a voice said to me, clear as day. "Kimberley, it's all going to be ok" and I felt the most amazing unconditional love. From that moment, I had faith.

In my deepest, darkest moments, I had faith. The little girl inside me always has faith. In the pits of drug addiction, I had faith, I knew that one day I would come through it and be free of the addiction. In the pits of darkness, my light shone.

This little light of mine, I'm going to let it shine! Always.

Following The Call of My Heart

When I started the seven-month Sentaura initiation process I was still living on Great Barrier Island, an island in the Hauraki Gulf, New Zealand. This is a very special place, the island has its own unique energy, and I received the nudge from Spirit to leave there and move back to the mainland, which I realised was perfect.

I packed everything and moved to North Auckland which was very close to the other two women who were also doing the Sentaura training, as well as Natali. This was totally meant to be, I felt part of a wonderful community of women and found a beautiful place to stay.

Rising Into the Light, a Deep Process

Natali asked us to keep a diary during the seven-month initiation program. Following are parts of the initiations as she led us through 24 transmissions guided by the Seraphim and various Cosmic Beings of Light, so you get an idea of the intensity, power, and amazingness of these initiations.

I will begin with the very first Sentaura pre-initiation, before the start of the training on 2nd July 2021, as this was important to me. Since I cannot draw here, it is best that I describe what I was given and saw. Looking back now, I am amazed at how much I have changed and how far I have come.

During this initiation I was given a beautiful diamond symbol that was multifaceted with a cross through it. Then from the Elves, a magnificent crown, which was again, multi-faceted that moved with my energy, as well as a staff with a blue teardrop crystal on the top, which helped me direct the element of water.

In my Sentaura training, I have been told various times about my ability to command and purify water. What an amazing ability! I see myself standing in the water and parting it using my energy. It was wonderful to sense this innate power within me, and it excites me to see how this will play out in my work as a healer.

I have always been drawn to the water. When I was two years old, I almost drowned in a trough on the farm where I lived. I was walking to my dad, who was working the land on the tractor, and I leaned into a trough too far and fell in. I now realise that this was because of my constant fascination with water. As I am tuning in now writing this chapter, I can feel the fairies very strongly around me, telling me that they saved me.

I was certainly protected and supported that day because my wonderful Dad told me the story of how he just intuitively knew that he had to get off the tractor and go back to the house at that very moment. On the way back he just happened to glance into the trough, and there I was, floating in the water. He rushed me to the shower and though my body was freezing to the touch, he brought me back to life.

I have a very special connection with my father, he always heard me when I would call him in my head when I was in bed scared and too frightened to yell out because I could feel spirits all around me. I would silently scream "Daddy" and pray that he would come, and he always would. He would pop his head around my bedroom door and say: "Everything ok Kimbles?". I would cry with relief and ask him for his warm hugs and assurance. He always accepted my requests and comforted me.

So, you can see how water has always been a very powerful part of my life. I have the ability to co-create with water.

In the first initiation, we worked with the Ankh symbol, and we went to a very sacred place, a golden temple—where I felt extremely looked after and protected, and felt a deeper connection between Natali, myself and the two other women who were in the program with me, than ever before.

We all drank out of a golden chalice of rainbow essence, which felt so delicious. I sipped it tentatively then gulped it down to receive this nourishing energy.

During the seven-month initiation program I felt so supported by Natali and my Spirit Team, and still do, even after completing the training, Sentaura has completely changed my life and is still changing my life. Through Natali's compassionate guidance and the frequency of Sentaura, I can now deal with whatever is thrown my way. I am no longer afraid of my shadows—I feel them, transmute them, and see through the BS! I love who I am!

I AM HEALER

I AM MIND READER

I AM LIGHT CODE BRINGER

I AM WATER WEAVER

I AM TREE WHISPERER

I AM GIFT ACTIVATOR

I AM ANIMAL COMMUNICATOR

I AM EARTH TRANSMUTER

Awakening The Goddess Within

One of the initiations was around upgrading our bodies and awakening the goddess within. I felt my cells vibrating at such a high energy as my crystalline body expanded. It felt like my cells were being cleansed and renewed and I was held by Mother Gaia. I could feel my body and womb calling me to rest. It was such an extremely calm and blissful feeling.

After this initiation I found my body craving high vibrational foods like fruit and vegetables. Throughout the program I found myself eating less and craving very specific food. Being able to listen to your body about what it needs is so important.

My Star Mother and Soul Family

Part of the Sentaura training, meant having one-on-one healing and mentoring sessions with Natali once a month. This particular healing session with Natali was extremely memorable. Archangel Raphael came into the space. Fire began rising within me, a deep remembrance.

Natali described a 'White Rose Woman' who came into the space, and she later called herself 'Star Mother'. This powerful woman was here to support and protect me through this process. She was the one who had been coming to me during visions for some time and told me: "Do not fear".

Have you heard of the Acturians? They are my soul family. I hold Arcturian soul codes, channel them through light language and feel them all around me frequently. I was not surprised when they came through in the healing session to assist me, clear my energy and bring through guidance.

During the session with Natali, we shifted a lot of old and unhelpful stories and energy. I let go of old parts of me and felt my true essence returning whilst claiming back lost parts of me. I felt these words rise within me:

I AM AMAZING, WISE, POWERFUL, PASSIONATE

I AM EVERYTHING FOR ME!

I CARE ABOUT ME

I MATTER

I AM ALWAYS SUPPORTED

I DESERVE TO HAVE THE VERY BEST!

The Wild Woman

During this initiation I felt more ready for the transmission than ever. I felt as if I had fully accepted who I was. After the first few initiations and my personal sessions with Natali I started being more aware of the voice that came through me. The voice that told me what I am not and what I can't do. Even now, I notice this much more and am able to sit with it, witness it and transmute it.

With each initiation I noticed how I would start releasing shadow parts of me even before the day of the initiation. What I found very interesting was that I had no idea that the next one would be around the womb and yoni consciousness, and two days earlier, I had a huge release around sexual abuse. It just goes to show that the upgrades, clearing and releases were all in the most perfect divine timing!

I felt amazing after this initiation. I could feel the essence of my goddess and wild woman so much more. I brought her forth in a new container of safety, love, compassion, forgiveness and truth. It felt so much healthier, more aligned. This brand-new container I created for me, filled with self-love, was epic.

During this initiation, Natali guided us to hold each other whilst each one of us separately received the Sentaura Code and it was so potent. An amazing pink and burgundy light surrounded me and brought forth my wild woman. I have known that I am a

Sister of the Rose for a long time and I could see myself wearing a huge crown, which was absolutely radiant.

The Abundance Code

I felt as if I was on a whirlwind of shifting and transmuting old patterns the day before this initiation. Natali showed us the Sentaura Key Code of Abundance™ which she channelled and then drew. It was absolutely beautiful. I cried deep tears of grief centuries old about losing love, being left by those I loved and pushing love away. What does this have to do with abundance? Abundance comes in many forms, ultimately abundance is within us and all around us, it is love.

My cat who came to me during the Sentaura program has been one of my biggest teachers. Teaching me about love, loosing love and letting go of attachment. Ten days after I brought him home from the rescue centre, he disappeared. I was distraught and thought: "Oh no not another love that has left me!" Three weeks later I surrendered, I thought he had gone forever and got rid of his food bowl and suddenly, he arrived back the next day! The lesson for me was to let go. You can't hang onto or own anything. Just love and if it is meant to be, it will.

The Fairies

The fairies showed me just how powerful they are and what they do working in co-creation with the elementals.

As a young girl of around five—yes everything seemed to happen to me at the age of five. I would speak to the fairies, they were my only friends. Growing up on a farm, with just me and my dad, I would amuse myself for hours in the flowers with the fairies. To me they represent pure joy, unconditional love, fun and happiness.

It is part of my life's purpose to work with the fairies, to share how they work with the world and what they do for us and the Earth. They showed me how they work with the elements to shift energy. Through Sentaura, I realised part of my purpose is to bring the truth about the fairies out to the world. Seeing the fairies and connecting with the fairies has been a huge blessing in my life.

You can imagine my delight when during our next initiation, the Fairy Queen came in and led the initiation transmitted through Natali. We went to many different levels in the Earth, and I was given a staff as a gift and to use as my magic wand so I could direct energies.

We were all given new frequencies to work with and Melchizedek shared his wisdom and enlightenment around my gift of telepathy.

I've always had the ability to intuitively know what someone was feeling and thinking. It has been both a blessing and an overwhelming gift to have, especially when I don't really want to hear other people's thoughts.

It has been a lesson of knowing what is mine and what is not. During the Sentaura program Natali taught us to fine tune our listening skills and telepathic abilities, to turn down the 'noise' when it got too much and to go within.

Before each initiation, we were directed by Spirit to work through releasing stories, limiting beliefs, patterns and most of these correlated to or matched the theme and frequency of the initiation and Sentaura Creator Key Code™.

I felt incredibly supported during each initiation and the whole training process. At the start of the program, I was wondering how I would afford this training though I never had any issues with money, it was always there for me and came easily to me throughout the whole seven months. I am a firm believer that if you are meant to do something and you are living your purpose and your dream, then the money is always there.

After a few months of working with Natali and receiving transmissions and initiations from her, I felt as if my life was about to take off in a major way.

After initiations plenty of rest and recalibration was required. I was excited to start working as a Sentaura Healer and to share what I have learned but also realised I had to be patient and continue my own inner work before I could truly help others.

At one point Natali tuned into my energy and told me that my third eye was completely expanded after the initiation. It meant that I could go deeper into other realms having expanded psychic vision. I could feel this expansion in my third eye as the night before, I guided my Lightworker Group through a wonderful meditation working with the fairies. I led them to the Fairy Kingdom through their Sacred Heart space. This felt incredibly easy, and I could see things in my mind's eye so clearly.

Rays of Light

One initiation and training session Natali took us through was all about the Emerald Ray, Amethyst Ray and Gold Ray. This was a potent session where we upgraded and re-balanced all our chakras and rose into higher realms. I could really see and feel the Golden Light of the Gold Ray permeating every single cell.

I started to believe in myself more than ever before. I have the belief now that nothing can affect me unless I choose to let it. I am in control of my life. My thoughts create my reality, and I am in charge of my thoughts.

Our Special Healing Place

This work with Sentaura is such a deep remembrance of what I already know. I know that we have all trained together before in another life.

What I loved about these initiations was that we gathered at different locations. Our favourite was Wenderholm, there is something truly magical about this place. There are many elementals and fairies there.

This specific initiation was with the Orion Beings which was being transmitted by Natali. All I can say is Wow! The next day, I could still feel these blue beings around me, and their energy felt like nothing I have ever encountered before. They were here to purify and cleanse what was not in alignment with our highest good and for our planet, and to open new neural pathways in our brain. We were now channelling cosmic wisdom in a completely different way.

In this initiation, they gently touched our heads and shoulders. Afterwards we all commented on how our heads felt different. It felt like we received a 'brain upgrade' and our heads felt much bigger.

The Sentaura initiations were intense but beautiful—they are not for the faint hearted. You might wonder why I say this? The loving frequency of Sentaura brings up everything you don't want to see, everything you have been hiding from and makes more space for love and light to flow through you. For the first six months, I felt a lot of dense energy being released. With each initiation however, I felt so much love, and a new level of courage and knew I had to trust that I was on the right path and that I was getting back to my true self more.

What I realised about myself is that I had a lot of trauma in my emotional body that has taken years to release. Being able to deal with my emotions is huge for me. To feel them, sit with them and transmute them more easily felt so good.

Upon completing the training, I dramatically started to see my life shift in such beautiful new ways. It was as if the seven-month initiations were preparing us for our new life, a new way of working with our own energy and a new way of working with other human beings, animals, plants, Mother Gaia and our Cosmic Family. Integration was a key part of the initiation process, and we were guided by Natali to rest, nourish and nurture ourselves in a very specific way.

I realised the power of integration and how my incredible body works. Due to my sensitive nature my body needs more time to integrate. So, giving myself integration time was probably the most challenging because I would expect immediate change and shifts, and I would get frustrated if things did not happen instantly.

What I've realised from doing this powerful work is that energy works instantly but you don't see shifts happening in the physical right away. My human needed time to integrate and my mind needed time to catch up, and most of the time I would only realise the huge shifts that happened for me a week later or months later. Having this awareness of integration time being a necessity is key.

I know that I needed to experience what I went through to prepare me for great things ahead and to bring me out of the darkness I experienced over many lives, and into the light once and for all. I had to face my shadows to truly see my light and to step into my power as a lightworker.

The loving frequency of Sentaura helps us to cut through all those past lives and realign ourselves to the timeline we are on now. As a lightworker I am here to work in the Light. Natali's work is integral to humanity evolving, and I believe one of the main purposes of the Sentaura frequency returning through her, is to bring Lightworkers back into the light and to align them with their highest truth and soul mission.

Working with Natali and the frequency of Sentaura she transmits has been an eye opener and I found my fear getting less and less. Now, when I reflect, it is gone.

What I realised quite quickly throughout my initiation process was that I am a powerful water weaver. What does this mean? I use light codes to shift energy and heal the water.

During some initiations I found myself weaving my hands, igniting ancient codes to heal specific things and shift energies. Working in co-creation with the elementals is powerful, especially working with the fairies and combining elemental energy.

The fairies come in when I work with the wind element. Have you ever started moving your hands in a certain way and didn't know why? This is a wonderful way to bring codes into your healing.

When I was growing up, my hands would often go very hot. Now I know why—it was when I activated the healing magic within me.

Through the work with Sentaura, my confidence to do things myself has grown immensely. I believe in my ability to now do things for myself. Of course, I need support and I am much better at asking for it now, but I am no longer a victim. I found that many old friends have fallen away, and many new friends and loving relationships have entered my life that I am worthy of, deserving of and which are healthy for me. Also, new powerful lightworker friends have entered my life, who I can relate to, be myself and have fun with.

New Guides

I had many new guides come to me during our initiations. One of them was a beautiful cheetah called Isabela and she came to me one night whilst I was sleeping. I could feel an enormous cat on the end of my bed. I didn't move a muscle, in fact I was a little scared because I could actually feel this cat kneading my foot, just like a cat does. I couldn't believe what I was feeling and decided to be brave and ask who it was. I instantly got the name Isabela (funnily enough, Isabela is the name of various of my guides, including my fairy). I was later told by my Guides that this was because in the different realms, names don't matter. The cheetah was sent to protect me. Now I have all the cats around me. I have a lion, cheetah, jaguar and a panther. They are part of my protection team.

I have such a strong connection with cats, have them as pets and have always loved them. They are such great companions and friends.

From a very young age, I realised I could talk to animals. Especially cats and over the years, dogs too. I hear them, like a thought and quite often my cat Velvet will say thank you to me for looking after him and providing him with food.

I do healing sessions and readings for pets and all I need is a photo to tune in, and they will immediately start talking to me.

My friend had a very sick cat, and it had a huge message for its owner. The cat was so relieved as she had been waiting to get this message across for some time.

One of my clients has a dog he loves dearly and during healing sessions with my client he always asks me to communicate with his dog to make sure she is happy. It is so beautiful to see their connection and the wonderful messages that come through.

Happy and Free

Now several months after the Sentaura Practitioner and Alchemist of Light training has finished, I am off my medication, sleeping well and without any need for any sleeping assistance. I'm constantly noticing the changes in my life and the changes I am making in other people's lives. My connection to my guides and the elementals is profound. I have a very special connection with the fairies, dragons and Pegasus.

I am more focused, I have clarity around my passions and where I want to go. I celebrate my uniqueness and no longer run away from being seen as 'different'. I love being me. I have my life back and am discovering more about myself each day. I decide who I want to hang around with and this is huge for me.

I know myself, I know my power, I feel my feminine essence and sexuality to a heightened level, all my fears have gone, all my sexual traumas, all my triggers that would not allow me to be fully present with my partner, have gone. It wasn't until I started experiencing all this joy that I realised how much I was missing and how afraid I was of my sexuality.

I feel like I have so much more space in my body, and I can fully slow down for the first time in my life and trust my body and what it needs and allow this.

One of the things Natali and Sentaura immensely assisted me with was sexual trauma. Feeling rejected was a huge issue for me and I had a lot of wounding around men, after experiencing numerous incidents of sexual abuse. It wasn't until I was in a relationship again, after integrating all the work I have done with Natali, that I realised my trauma had gone.

When I met a wonderful new partner and started being my full sensual self, I realised how shut off and afraid I had been to express myself in intimacy. Now all of my desires are being realised, I feel a magical energy within me, a thirst for life and all the wonderful things it has ignited within me. In fact, my whole sexual self changed and I realised what my true self was actually craving and I accepted it, wholly and completely.

The Sentaura frequency and all the energies it transmits are so potent. I have learned how to manage my energy, so my human body and nervous system has time to recalibrate. I have really had to learn to just let healing integrate before I do more. I also only stick to using Kinesiology and working with the frequency of Sentaura now.

I Will Forever Be Grateful for This Woman

Natali is the most compassionate person I have ever met. What I was going through was so intense that I needed a lot of support. Prior to working with Natali, I never had a mentor who has been so patient and kind to me and willing to 'kick me up the butt' when I needed it.

It was those kicks up the butt that got me to where I am today, along with her devotion, friendship and love. I cannot express the amount of gratitude I have for Natali. Not only is she the most honourable and strongest woman I know, but she has also brought me back into myself more times than I can count. She has the most immense trust and belief in me, and it has assisted me to believe in myself as a lightworker, healer and goddess.

At times, I have relied so greatly on Natali, and it has been a long road, because she is a light that shines so brightly, and she has enabled me to step into my own power and open my own wings. Bringing Sentaura to this world has been an incredible journey for Natali but I am so glad she did because the work with Sentaura has given me the strength to be truly myself.

The amount of strength that I received from Sentaura, and the purity of the light transmitted through Natali and Sentaura is so immense. I know that I am always protected because I have a special job to do for humanity. Even when times are tough and I need support as a healer, Natali is always there. She is a healer and way shower for the healers.

My heart is so full of love for her and for what she is doing for humanity. It takes extreme bravery and commitment to do what she does. I am so proud.

How I combine Kinesiology with Sentaura Healing

I have been in a clinic space for over a decade, using Kinesiology as a powerful tool to shift energy, bring forth change, create new belief systems and shift obstacles for people. Now that I merge Sentaura Ascension Energy Healing and Kinesiology, the potency of my sessions has increased dramatically.

Muscle testing is extremely powerful and through my Kinesiology training, I was using a very specific protocol to check for imbalances and stresses in the body before and during my sessions. However, once I started combining Sentaura Energy Healing with my Kinesiology sessions, I no longer have to do all the pre-checks on the body, as Sentaura is doing it for me.

The way my sessions are run have changed dramatically, I no longer have to do all the work I was having to do, using Sentaura has shortened my process so I can focus more on getting deeper into the healing and shifting trauma, fear and belief systems.

Having a session with me means deep clearing on a personal level. Sentaura amplifies my ability to see exactly what is going on in the psyche and energy system. I activated a special gift to use my vision like an x-ray and see what is going on in the body and the shifts that need to happen.

My hands move as I work through the body's systems, speaking light language. One of my clients said that he saw a serpent being removed as I was using my language and whilst bringing through codes of light.

Whilst working with a client and channelling Sentaura, I felt another energy come in—it was the dragons and was a first for me. To feel the dragon energy coming through me so powerfully was as if I was the dragon, I could feel my wings and the strength of the dragons.

When I first started working with the frequency of Sentaura, I would feel very dizzy and lightheaded afterwards because the frequency transmitted by Natali was so potent and incredibly high frequency.

But as I adjusted to the frequency, I felt less and less affected by it, because my body was recalibrated to hold more light. Now when I work with Sentaura, I feel much stronger and able to hold the frequency for so much longer. Now I call in Sentaura and it just feels like it's part of me.

I have learned so much from my experiences and I am so grateful that I get to help others through my own learnings and experiences. I now teach from my own experiences.

Earth Healing

As part of our Sentaura training we do Earth healing and are given specific missions by Spirit, guided by Natali, to assist the ascension journey of our Earth and humanity. We regularly get together in our Sentaura Healers Community and I feel so blessed to be with a group of wonderful healers to do this incredibly important work with—it feels like such a sacred space to be in. It is pure magic, unconditional love and joy!

One of the things I did want to mention is that since I have been doing Earth Healings and continuously receiving upgrades, initiations, and healing sessions with Natali, I have the ability to energetically be in more than one place at a time.

It started during one of our recent Earth Healings with the new group of Sentaura students. Usually, Natali guides us where to go as she receives transmissions and messages from her Spirit Team.

Once I connect to the group my higher self takes me to where I need to be, and I do the work that is needed. However, this time I went to one place, then suddenly I saw myself go to several different locations and places, and on it went, until I was at around a hundred different places all at once!

I could see all the different versions of me coming from my original self and going to different locations whilst doing healing and clearing work. I had never experienced anything like it. Now

I know I have an incredible ability to be in more than one place at a time.

Since then, I have had to really work on keeping myself grounded and ensuring I call back all parts of me. Even though I know that on a multi-dimensional level, in particular, in my sleep, I am always working, which is why rest is so important for me.

Talking of rest, boy do you need it with the Sentaura work. After most Earth healing sessions, I would feel exhausted but all it took was a little shut eye, sometimes only ten minutes, and I would feel right as rain.

I have learned how to pace myself and to regulate my energy. My body does not like any stimulants although you can't beat a bit of chocolate after doing Sentaura work, it helps you ground.

We went on earth healing missions to clear and purify the water. This was my favourite part of the Earth Healing because I am a water weaver and felt deeply connected and in my power throughout this. During one of these Earth healing sessions, I saw myself with glorious long hair under the water using light language, singing a beautiful melody and purifying the water! It was so beautiful!

The Alchemic Dance Floor

I am also an Ecstatic Dance DJ, train new DJ students and run dance conscious events bringing joy to others through music and dance. Since Sentaura my work as a DJ has gone off the hook! I created Alchemic Dance Floor and when DJing I can feel the energy of Sentaura amplify the frequency of the music and within me, and huge transformation happen for people on the dance floor during my events. I DJ at various other venues, and each time before I DJ, I set up the space doing what I learned during the Sentaura Practitioner Program so those who want to receive healing in that space will receive it for their highest greatest good whilst they dance to my tunes. Cool huh!

Sentaura Changed my Life

Before I found Natali and Sentaura, I would book one to three different healing sessions per week with other healers. I was constantly searching for ways to fix myself and felt deeply broken inside. I thought I needed help all the time to shift my stuff. Even though I had been confidently assisting other people for years and knew exactly how to help them, I still didn't feel powerful enough to fully clear my own trauma. Yes sure, I would work on myself, but I had low self-esteem and felt there was always something wrong with me. Yikes, what a way to live!

I would go to conscious festivals where there were workshops on self-improvement and I would go to as many as I could and receive as much healing as I could, all whilst running a DJ set, performing to a huge crowd and running workshops. I would leave the festivals on a high, but would quickly come down and feel scattered because I had absorbed so much information and energy and did not give myself the time I needed in between sessions to integrate.

Since I completed the Sentaura Healing Practitioner Training, all I use is Kinesiology and Sentaura healing energy—it is all there is. There is no other frequency I wish to work with as Sentaura is God's Creator Frequency. God's energy assists me and guides me every single day. I no longer have the cravings and addictions to 'fix' myself and no longer have the need to see so many therapists, practitioners, and healers. Because all I need is to trust and believe in myself.

The frequency of Sentaura is the highest, purest source frequency available to humanity which transmits and holds all frequencies and organic technologies within it. It is so different from any other modalities. Its frequency cannot be matched or recreated in any way. It is such a relief to simplify my life and use just one way of healing, clearing, upgrading, and recalibrating energy as this truly works for me! I am living and breathing this work, it feels so easy.

Another thing I have learned during my training is the importance of clearing your energy field every day and making this part of your practice. This has changed my life dramatically.

I use the Blue Sirian Energy and Pyramid of Light that Natali told us to use to purify my body and strengthen my energy. I love teaching my clients how to cleanse their energy as we are energy beings in human form, and this is so important. Whenever I go anywhere, I have my spirit team with me, and I call a powerful pyramid of light around me. I see myself surrounded by the blue light of the Sirians and the energy of Archangel Michael, a powerful protection energy.

My trust in myself and my abilities increased tenfold. I trust my team has got my back. I trust that I am safe and protected. I trust that anything happening is to make me stronger and prepare me for my journey ahead. I trust that I am always looked after.

Having an abundance mentality is so powerful. My firm belief is that if you are meant to do something, you will be given all the funds to do it! So, once I committed to doing Sentaura, the money was there. It has been like this for all my training. Of course, taking action is necessary. Once you commit to yourself and your journey then you are always supported.

Now I celebrate myself so much more.

Every day I celebrate who I am and my wellness.

I celebrate being alive, well and brave.

Having faith in yourself is so important.

Faith has got me through everything!!

Who am I? I had to learn how to look after myself first and along the way I am finding more of me. I know I am a lightworker, healer, water weaver and courageous woman. I love assisting and guiding others on their healing journey, it is my purpose.

I now know my 'f*ck yes' and 'f*ck no'. I have established clear boundaries and can clearly see through any bullsh*t. I can tell right away when someone is not truthful and am getting much better at listening to that body response. Because if I don't, I can feel a physical response to this untruth in my body.

Sentaura helped me access my quirky, funny self once again! I love my life, my cat, fairies and unicorns. I love saying 'meow' to all my friends and now they love saying it back to me. It's fun and I love it!

Here are case studies of Sentaura Healing Sessions I've done for clients:

Mould Client

This client came to me initially because she had an issue with mould. She had an overgrowth of mould in the body and was on medication to reduce the mould. She so wanted to have a baby and to fall pregnant to her long-term partner. However, the doctors advised her to not fall pregnant while she was on medication for mould overgrowth.

When I tuned into her body, I could see the mould as darkness and dark shadows. I called in Sentaura and started transmitting a powerful frequency directing it into her body and could see myself literally zapping the mould. It was the most powerful and intense energy I've ever felt come through me.

That day we focused on clearing the mould from her body. Then through Kinesiology we started focusing on belief systems she had around having a baby.

She continued to have three more sessions with the same intention to clear the mould from her body. I was guided by my team of light that she needed three initial sessions, then to continue working with her periodically to keep the vibration of her body high and clear out any density.

On the fourth session she came to me excited because she had been to see her Holistic Doctor who had muscle tested her and the mould was completely gone from her body! He was surprised and asked her how this happened. She advised him, it happened energetically!

This meant that she could come off her mould medication. We continued our work and energetically cleared past lives, where she was a mother of seven and didn't want any more children. From her womb we cleared the energetic imprint of a child she had lost in another life and cleared beliefs about being deserving of being a mother. We cleared cords and attachments from her own mother line and energies that were draining her life force.

Within five months of her initially coming to see me, she fell pregnant! I knew immediately as she walked into my clinic room. I could sense the change in her energy field, and she was so excited.

However, there was still more work to do with her because she was feeling excited but also didn't feel the joy that she was expecting. I am continuing working with her, to shift old mood patterns, allowing her to feel like a pregnant sexy goddess! As we continue working together, I am seeing immense change in her behaviour, energy field, emotional body, pain body and in her overall health.

Sexual Trauma Client

During NZ Spirit Festival Natali decided to run a workshop there on Sentaura Cosmic Ascension Energy so other people could experience. We held space during the workshop and were walking around the space and being guided by Sentaura to facilitate healing for those in the tent. There was one woman who I felt extremely drawn to and I was immediately guided to her womb space. I gently put my hand on her womb and felt so much emotion being released and felt her whole energy shift. When I looked at her, I could see there were tears flowing down her face. I knew I had just tapped into some very deep and old trauma. I spoke light language and transmuted the energy that needed to be shifted for her highest greatest good. I knew that something huge had been shifted for her.

It didn't surprise me that at the end of the workshop, she approached me and told me how she had felt a huge shift and that I had tapped into something very deep for her.

Spirit advised me that our work was not yet complete, and I would be seeing her again. I told her and she agreed that she would like to see me again when the time was right. She felt there was a huge synchronicity to us meeting.

Sentaura brings about magical happenings like this!

So, when I saw her again a couple of months later, she advised me that she had felt so shut off from her relationship and she wanted to feel happy again. It was very difficult for her to connect to any feminine space within her.

She had felt blockages in her womb space, mostly because of sexual trauma and mother-daughter disconnect from upbringing.

During Sentaura Healing, I could feel a man's presence still in her energetic field. He was still having control over her life and keeping her in a space of terror. It felt easy to shift this, because with Sentaura and my team, it just gets released through my codes and light language and by simply asking for it to go. Sentaura amplifies your power of awareness, and its source intelligence guides you throughout the whole healing process.

The session was incredibly potent and magical and further womb clearings happened.

She wrote me a beautiful testimonial:

"As Kimberley focused on my body and spirit, I could really feel her extract the toxic energy that was leached onto my field. It was such an emotional, beautiful transition coming from a loud, anxious headspace to complete still, nothingness. This has been a space that I have really ached for, for peace, for control of my thoughts and anxieties."

She claimed back her power and it enabled her to feel more in control of her life. This is what I do, I help you go from feeling powerless to feeling free and sovereign.

The Poisoned Dog

One of my favourite clients has a dog that he just adores. One day he messaged me in a panic because his dog was at the vet with something terribly wrong that they couldn't figure out. They thought that perhaps she had eaten something poisonous. I offered to assist and remotely tuned in to see what was going on.

When I tuned in using Sentaura and my guides, I saw a dense matter in her stomach, which I energetically removed. I was then guided to remove something from her throat, which I pulled out and was guided to heal her teeth. It was a short but very potent and powerful session.

The next day, I heard from my client who advised me that she was back from the vet and in perfect health. The vet couldn't figure out how she recovered so quickly. Working with Sentaura in this way made me smile.

Working with Sentaura is Truly Fulfilling

My Sentaura training has been nothing short of brilliant, life changing and magnificent. The things I have experienced, Natali's transmissions, healing and teachings are phenomenal. I highly recommend Sentaura, and the work Natali does for the world. I would love the whole world to experience the loving Frequency of Sentaura.

I believe in myself more than ever and love the work I do. Helping others to heal, share the loving frequency of Sentaura and use all I learned is truly fulfilling.

Each healing experience is so different and uplifting. As I heal others, I also receive healing and learn so much from the beings that support each healing session. This beautiful frequency teaches me so much about self-worth, acceptance and determination.

Live and Love your Life. Realise your Self Worth and most importantly, Be You!

You are here to live a unique life on this planet. Embrace it!

Love, Kimberley Jade

KIMBERLEY JADE PIPE

ABOUT THE AUTHOR

Kimberley Jade Pipe is an empowered healer and teacher using the multi-dimensional frequency of Sentaura combined with Kinesiology as a tool to shift energy, facilitate healing and transformation for her clients. She assists people to step into their power by clearing blockages and self-sabotaging beliefs so they may release fear, pain and trauma.

She weaves her love of music into teaching DJ training, facilitating Ecstatic Dance and letting the frequency of music fill the hearts of those she works with.

She helps people reconnect back to the love and the joy within enabling them to create new and more positive beliefs for themselves.

She lives in Auckland, New Zealand with her cat Velvet. She loves animals particularly cats, playing the bass guitar, roller blading and surfing.

Website:
https://www.jadeenergies.com/

Facebook – Jade Energies:
https://www.facebook.com/jade.energies

Facebook – Kimba DJ:
https://www.facebook.com/kimbadj

Instagram:
https://www.instagram.com/djkimbajade/

Dedicated To

Our Creator and our Guides from the Highest Light and Love

To our family, friends and teachers and all who follow our work. Thank you for your love, guidance, celebration and support.

Our hearts overflow with gratitude, always.

For Mum, Pippin and Ellie the Cat, Oumas and Oupas, I miss you and love you forever. To Dad, thank you for believing in me and for always supporting me.

xxx

Dedicated to my legendary Mum and Dad, thank you for always believing in me, I miss you both every day, lots & lots of love forever in my heart. Gx

xxx

Much gratitude to my biggest supporter and client, my Mum and in remembrance of Jimmy, thank you

xxx

Much gratitude to Dad for always having my back, accepting me and supporting me in all my endeavours, as whacky as they may be!

xxx

Write A Review

If you loved this book or received thought provoking insights from it, we would really appreciate it if you could leave a 30 second review on Amazon HERE: https://www.amazon.com/review/create-review?isbn=978-0473654894

www.ingramcontent.com/pod-product-compliance
Lightning Source LLC
Chambersburg PA
CBHW062032290426
44109CB00026B/2608